In a day in which an epidemic of character-depleted Christians are failing to impact our culture, Charlie Dyer has the "cure." His prescription for personal integrity will produce healthy believers whose Christianity will be contagious. *The Power of Personal Integrity* is just what the doctor ordered!

Dr. Steven J. Lawson
Senior Pastor, Dauphin Way Baptist Church
Author of Men Who Win

George Washington once said, "Few men have integrity to withstand the highest bidder," a colossal barrier that chokes our effectiveness in human relationships. Charlie Dyer has cut through this obstacle with a path to personal integrity from the Holy Scriptures. Here is a book that should be required reading for every student, from prep students to senior seminarians. None of us ever outgrows our need for a review of this essential lifetime subject.

Howard G. Hendricks
Distinguished Professor; Chairman, Center for Christian Leadership
Dallas Theological Seminary

This book is a stone. To be more precise, it's a whetstone. As you interact with the concepts in this book, you will be sharpening the blade of your personal integrity on the whetstone of biblical truth. My integrity edge was sharper when I finished this book; I think yours will be, too.

Steve Farrar
Men's Leadership Ministries; Author of Point Man

God desires to reproduce the life of Christ in every believer. By examining the lives of biblical characters who exemplified aspects of godliness and by studying the pertinent passages of Scripture, the author, in a clear, concise, convincing, and often in a convicting way, sets forth the qualities which characterize a godly life. A must for those who desire to fulfill God's will for their lives, "even [our] sanctification" (1 Thessalonians 4:3).

J. Dwight Pentecost
Distinguished Professor of Bible Exposition, Emeritus
Dallas Theological Seminary

Charlie Dyer has artfully mixed reflection and action, Scripture and relevance, theory and reality to produce a combat manual for those who battle with maintaining personal integrity. As he processes contemporary options to moral compromise through the eternal grid of the Bible, we learn that the issues are not that new after all. God's prescriptions stand for us now as they did when they were written.

Ramesh Richard
President, RREACH International;
Professor of Pastoral Ministries and World Missions and Intercultural Studies
Dallas Theological Seminary

The POWER of PERSONAL INTEGRITY

CHARLES DYER

Tyndale House Publishers, Inc.

WHEATON, ILLINOIS

Visit Tyndale's exciting Web site at www.tyndale.com

Unless otherwise indicated, all Scripture quotations are taken from the *Holy Bible,* New Living Translation, copyright © 1996. Used by permission of Tyndale House Publishers, Inc., Wheaton, Illinois 60189. All rights reserved.

Scripture quotations marked NIV are taken from the *Holy Bible,* New International Version®. NIV®. Copyright © 1973, 1978, 1984 by International Bible Society. Used by permission of Zondervan Publishing House. All rights reserved.

Scripture quotations marked KJV are taken from the *Holy Bible,* King James Version.

Library of Congress Cataloging-in-Publication Data

Dyer, Charles H., date
    The power of personal integrity / Charles Dyer.
      p. cm.
    ISBN 0-8423-4884-0 (pbk.)
    1. Integrity—Religious aspects—Christianity. I. Title.
BV4647.I55D84   1997
241'.4—DC20   96-43750

Printed in the United States of America

03 02 01 00 99 98 97
7   6   5   4   3   2

This book is dedicated to
Kay and Charlie Dyer,
who continue to model integrity to their children
. . . and grandchildren.

My son, obey your father's commands,
and don't neglect your mother's teaching.
Keep their words always in your heart.
Tie them around your neck.
Wherever you walk,
their counsel can lead you.
When you sleep, they will protect you.
When you wake up in the morning,
they will advise you.

PROVERBS 6:20-22

CONTENTS

FOREWORD *by Charles R. Swindoll* ix

INTRODUCTION xiii

1. HONESTY: *Is Honesty the Best Policy?* 1

2. COMPASSION: *Do Nice Guys Finish Last?* 21

3. WISDOM: *Are You Some Kind of Wise Guy?* 41

4. SELF-CONTROL: *If My Spirit Is Willing,
Why Is My Flesh So Weak?* 67

5. JOY: *Is Laughter the Best Medicine?* 83

6. TRUST: *Can I Depend on God?* 101

7. FAITHFULNESS: *Can God Depend on Me?* 119

8. BALANCE: *Does All Work and No Play Make Jack a Dull Boy?* 143

9. SEXUAL PURITY: *If It Feels Good, Why Not Do It?* 165

10. ENDURANCE: *How Do I Develop Spiritual Stamina?* 193

EPILOGUE 219

NOTES 227

FOREWORD

In 1973 Dr. Karl Menninger shocked his psychologist colleagues by using the *S* word in the title of his best-seller *Whatever Became of Sin?* For the first time, many of his readers were confronted with a word—and a concept—that had all but disappeared from their profession.

In its May 25, 1987, cover story, *Time* magazine asked another probing question: "What Ever Happened to Ethics?" By then, scandals had become the order of the day. They still are. It seems that no place remains sacred any longer: not the Oval Office at the White House or the Pentagon or Capitol Hill or NASA or Wall Street or the sports arena or the halls of academe or the medical and legal professions or, for that matter, the whole world of religion. We have lived through Watergate, Koreagate, Irangate, and even "Pearlygate," much to the embarrassment of Christians.

The psalmist's words have never been more relevant:

We are mocked by our neighbors, an object of scorn and derision to those around us. (Psalm 79:4)

With the disappearance of sin and the subsequent absence of ethics, no one should be surprised that absolutes of right and wrong have now been replaced by a gray foggy mixture of uncertainty and inconsistency. Look deep enough, search far enough, stay at it long enough, and skeletons begin to rattle from the closet of almost everyone's past. Few are the heroes who can withstand the laserlike probe of today's media examiners. How the mighty are fallen!

What's missing? What do we long to find at the core of those we admire? Integrity. And what is that?

My *Oxford English Dictionary* tells me the word is derived from the Latin *integritas,* which means "wholeness . . . completeness." The root term, *integer,* means "untouched, intact, entire." One with integrity is solid, authentic, upright. Interestingly, the Hebrew term usually translated "integrity" in the Old Testament *(tome)* means the same thing: "whole, complete, upright, ethically sound."

In light of that, it seems to me that what we need most is not more emphasis on the problem but greater insight into the solution. We don't need more heartbreaking stories of scandalous lives but reliable and forthright information on how to live differently in a world that's lost its way. It's time for someone to answer the real question: What ever can be done about integrity?

I have good news! That is precisely what my close personal friend and colleague Dr. Charles Dyer has done. In this volume, *The Power of Personal Integrity,* Charlie has not only addressed the need for integrity in a compelling manner, he's also helped us understand its component traits—like honesty, compassion, wisdom, self-control, joy, trust, faithfulness, sexual purity, and other equally significant dimensions of an authentic lifestyle.

I heartily recommend this book! You will find these three essentials here that make it worth your time:

1. It is interesting. You'll be drawn into the stories he tells and the scenes he paints.
2. It is biblical. Again and again, you will return to the Scriptures as a foundation is built and principles are formed.
3. It is resourceful. These pages are not merely the opinion of an author; they are also helpful, insightful thoughts that add depth to the discussion.

Best of all, the one who writes of integrity has been a consistent model of it for years. I know, having witnessed it over the long haul in situations where it has been put to the test. On each occasion, Charlie Dyer passed with flying colors.

I would make two suggestions before you begin to read *The Power of Personal Integrity.* First, from the start, read slowly and carefully. Second, when you finish, ask yourself, "What Ever Happened to Integrity *in Me?*"

Charles R. Swindoll
President, Dallas
Theological Seminary;
Bible Teacher,
Insight for Living

INTRODUCTION

Tuffy Toussaint

Garrison Keillor put Lake Wobegon, Minnesota, on the map! He made his radio listeners feel like honorary citizens of this mythical town "where all the women are strong, all the men are good looking, and all the children are above average." But Lake Wobegon existed only in Garrison Keillor's fertile mind. Hinckley, Minnesota, however, does exist—and its influence stretched into the classrooms of Dallas Theological Seminary through the words and actions of its number one booster: Stan Toussaint.

Stan served for many years as chairman of the Bible Exposition Department at Dallas Theological Seminary. His personality parallels that of Garrison Keillor. Infectious humor. Verbal precision. Keen intellect carefully hidden beneath homespun humor. A struggle with polio gave Stan a permanent limp, but the disease couldn't slow down this dynamo.

"Tuffy" Toussaint! I remember his deep laugh when he

told me that was the nickname students had given him when he first began teaching. They thought he didn't know! No one who ever sat under Stan's teaching ministry can forget his knowledge of God's Word, his ability to teach with clarity and relevance—and his humor.

Ask someone who studied under Stan Toussaint to quote his favorite phrase, and they will respond, "Great honks! Stone the crows and starve the lizards!" (Translation: "This could be important!")

I *love* Stan's preaching. I *laugh* at Stan's jokes. I *learn* when Stan teaches God's Word. But I *long* to reproduce Stan's character in my own life. He has a genuineness in his spiritual life, a sense of authenticity, that is compelling and convincing. When I spend time with Stan, I leave as a better person. What makes him so special? In a word: *integrity.*

Integrity is an idea everyone embraces but few can define—an ideal all believe in but few achieve. Chuck Swindoll latched onto the essence of integrity in his foreword. He said integrity refers to one who is "solid, authentic, upright." That's Stan Toussaint!

When conducting topographical surveys, the ability to establish points of reference is essential. Surveyors search for enduring objects, like rock outcroppings, that they can use as benchmarks—fixed signposts that help establish elevation. In the same way, we search out God's benchmarks—his fixed points that help us determine our level of personal integrity. And we discover these points of reference in the Bible.

Biblically, the word *integrity* describes someone whose

words and actions match God's written standards. A person of integrity is someone whose talk—and walk—resemble the character and conduct of Jesus Christ. In my mental dictionary, Stan Toussaint's picture appears beside the definition of integrity. I know integrity when I see it—and I see it in Stan Toussaint.

We Know It When We See It

My parents just bought a winter home in Florida. Actually, it's a modular home in a retirement village—but for them it is the perfect haven during the cold winter months. They both wanted a house that was very economical and low maintenance. No exterior to paint. No yard to mow. No weeds to pull.

To keep from having to mow the lawn, Mom and Dad put black plastic over the entire yard and then covered the plastic with white decorative stones. *Tons* of stones! Walk by their house on a foggy morning and you might think Florida had had a freak snowstorm. The entire yard glistens in white.

The first time I had the opportunity to visit their new home, as we drove through the streets of the retirement community, I kept watching. I didn't know the street number or the color of their house—so I watched for white rocks. And then the house came into view. I immediately recognized it because of the white rocks.

That same principle is true of integrity. Though we might stumble over definitions, intuitively we know integrity when we see it in action—modeled in the life of an individual. We study God's Word in our leather-bound

Bibles—but sometimes we grasp the truth of that Word more clearly when we see it wearing shoe leather. Never underestimate the power of a personal example, a flesh-and-blood illustration of personal integrity.

God understands this principle, and that's why so much of the Bible tells God's truth through the lives of people. Want to learn how to be wise? Walk with Solomon through the wise—and foolish—steps of his life. Struggling with faith? Travel in Abraham's caravan and watch his faith take shape and deepen. Concerned that your life is out of balance? Visit the home of Mary and Martha and observe these two women struggling to maintain balance during the stress points of their lives.

Why Another Book?

Solomon spent much of his life observing, collecting, reflecting—and writing on wisdom. He read it all, heard it all, and remembered it all. And his evaluation of most of what he had read is not flattering. "There is no end of opinions ready to be expressed. Studying them can go on forever and become very exhausting!" (Ecclesiastes 12:12). Ouch! So why write another book—even if the purpose is to focus on a subject as significant as integrity? I see two reasons.

First, Solomon did not condemn all writing—only writing that failed to promote wise living. In contrast to those books that do nothing but weary the reader, Solomon praised the words that come from God. "A wise teacher's words spur students to action and emphasize important truths. The collected sayings of the wise are like guidance from a shepherd" (12:11). God's truth is beneficial—his words are worth reading. And the purpose of *this* book is to help you understand more clearly *the* Book.

Second, I'm convinced that we need another book on personal integrity because our society is quickly losing its moral anchor. Those basic values we took for granted twenty years ago—values like honesty, purity, and faithfulness—are now questioned by many, including some who are sitting in church pews! Society is adrift and floating ever closer to the rocky shores of moral and spiritual catastrophe. Some have already suffered shipwreck. This book will encourage you, exhort you—and sometimes prod you—to a greater commitment to personal integrity.

Pack your suitcase, grab your passport, and come with me to visit some of the most fascinating people who inhabit the pages of the Bible! But before you begin, pause and ask God to give you an understanding mind and a sensitive heart. My prayer for you matches that of Paul for his friends at the church in Ephesus. "I pray for you constantly, asking God, the glorious Father of our Lord Jesus Christ, to give you spiritual wisdom and understanding, so that you might grow in your knowledge of God" (Ephesians 1:16-17).

1

HONESTY

Is Honesty the Best Policy?

Looking for an Honest Person

Travel back through time over 2,300 years to Athens in the fourth century B.C. As you wind through the stone streets of the city, the bright light of the sun casts harsh shadows on the stone pathway before you. You make your way through these mottled streets from the marketplace to your home, carrying your meager purchases for tonight's meal in a small sack by your side.

As you round a corner, you spot a man in the distance carrying a lighted lamp. How odd! Why is he carrying a lamp when the sun is so bright? You watch as he pushes the lamp into the faces of oncoming pedestrians. He draws closer, and now you make out the simple dress and bare feet of this walking lamppost. He is almost beside you before his shaking hands thrust the clay lamp into your face. Then he asks his penetrating question: "Are you an honest person?"

Meet Diogenes—the Greek philosopher asking uncomfortable questions. Diogenes belonged to the *Cynic* school of philosophy, whose members believed virtue was the only good. They sought the essence of good in self-control and independence. In looking for an honest individual, Diogenes searched for someone not motivated by self-interest.

You are made strangely uncomfortable by his penetrating eyes and abrupt question. Does he know about you? You hesitate but a moment before answering, but even as you begin to speak you are sure he notices the catch in your voice. He moves on in his search for someone honest, and you head home, pondering the emptiness of your answer.

Today the world still has a surplus of cynics and a shortage of honest individuals. Were Diogenes walking the streets of our cities, he would be more likely to be mugged or arrested than to be successful in his search. Honesty is still a rare commodity.

I thank God that Diogenes wasn't walking the streets of my hometown in the late 1950s. W. F. Woolworth anchored the strategic "kids' corner" on Main Street. Down one street was the Columbia Movie Theater, while across the other street stood the Capitol Movie House. There, nestled between Saturday's matinees, stood the treasure-house of trinkets—the store that had it all! Just inside the front entrance, to the left of the main aisle, was the candy counter. A vast selection of chocolate candies and assorted nuts filled the bins around its edge.

It's funny how little events can traumatize us. I remember walking past the display, the wooden floor creaking under my small feet. The corner bin was filled with cashews. The smell of the hot oil mixed with the roasted nuts was just too great. My tiny hand reached quickly from the bin to my mouth, and a single cashew made its disappearing act.

"Hey, did you just take a cashew?" a gruff voice shouted from behind the counter. "Me? No!" I lied, holding the cashew like a chaw of tobacco between my cheek and gum. "I saw you take it!" he shot back. I vehemently protested my innocence all the while my little feet shuffled toward the door. I'm sure the cashier had trouble understanding me with a half-eaten cashew stuck to the side of my suddenly dry mouth.

To the best of my knowledge, I had never tasted a cashew before that theft at Woolworth's. But for years afterward I couldn't bring myself to eat a cashew. Even today, the taste of a cashew brings with it vivid memories of a life of crime nipped in the bud by a blustering cashier and a bitter cashew.

The Pro Bowl of Liars

If lying were a sport and fans could nominate the best for the Pro Bowl of Liars, three specific groups of individuals would always lead the fans' list of nominees: televangelists, used-car salesmen, and politicians. Why do we think of these three groups when the subject of honesty comes up?

TELEVANGELISTS

Televangelists claim to be men or women of God. And most are. At their best they stand as modern-day prophets, denouncing sin and calling their listeners to a closer walk with God. They also ask their audience to share financially to further the ministry. Unfortunately, the past few years have not been good ones for televangelists. Some betrayed this trust. Criminal investigations exposed their lavish lifestyles and sexual sins to the public. Hypocrites! Frauds! Charlatans! And a cynical world painted many sincere, honest ministries with the same brush of criticism because of those few who lacked honesty. But if we view televangelists with suspicion, we treat used-car salesmen with outright skepticism and distrust.

USED-CAR SALESMEN

Used-car salesmen are the butt of many jokes. The punch line usually focuses on their greed or dishonesty. Why is this particular occupation so maligned? Can you imagine the following conversation with a used-car salesman?

> **Customer:** She looks great! But what about safety?
>
> **Salesman:** Well, actually the car is nothing but plastic. Back into a pole at five miles per hour and your bumper and fender will shatter. It will set you back nearly seven hundred dollars.
>
> **Customer:** But is this particular model reliable?
>
> **Salesman:** The car was warranteed for three years or 36,000 miles. This particular used car had 30,000 miles on the odometer, but we rolled it back 10,000. Plan on replacing the air-conditioning condenser in about six months. And your transmission has plastic parts that ought to wear out about a year later.

Customer: I find what you are saying very disturbing. In all honesty, would you buy this car?

Salesman: Frankly, if it were my decision I wouldn't own this car on a bet!

Most used-car salesmen will ignore, overlook, or disregard potential problems in the automobiles they are trying to sell. But before you become too righteous in your indignation, how many flaws did you point out in the last automobile you traded in? Did you tell the salesman about the oil leak, the rattle in the transmission, the vibration in the front end that begins when the car reaches fifty miles per hour?

POLITICIANS

We distrust politicians because some (not all!) make outrageous promises that they cannot possibly keep in order to get elected. We all learn very early not to trust the "promises" of politicians.

While growing up, I went to Boy Scout camp every summer. Each year we held elections for the Water Carnival King. Usually each troop nominated a nonswimmer from their group to run for this valued office. Campaigning was vigorous, and promises spewed from the lips of the wanna-be kings. An annual favorite was the promise to install fur-lined toilet seats in the unheated latrines. The winner never honored his campaign promises, nor did we expect him to. After all, this was like other elections!

Michael Kelly wrote a candid assessment of President Clinton, and his words could easily apply to most presidents and politicians. "In mainstream journalism and even more so in popular entertainment, President Clinton is routinely depicted as a liar, a fraud, an indecisive man who can't be trusted to stand for anything—or with anyone." Kelly goes on to write of "the everyday acts of minor corruption and falsity that the business of politics demands."[1]

Politicians are not any more evil or corrupt than society as a whole. They are simply under more scrutiny because the promises they make are public. We entrust our leaders with the authority to do what is right, but then they face added temptations that come with being part of the power structure. Edmund Burke wrote, "The greater the power, the more dangerous the abuse," and that is a danger faced by all politicians.

Gini Graham Scott, a psychologist and author, has studied the problem of lying in our society. The product of her research is a book entitled *The Truth about Lying.* In an interview with Barbara De Witt, Ms. Scott shared about the growing tendency to lie in our society. "Lying is becoming a threat to our society. It's gone beyond a certain point, where people can no longer trust each other."[2]

An Honest Politician

Had Diogenes lived two centuries earlier, he could have found his honest man. And that honest man was a career politician! His name at birth was Daniel, which means "God is my judge." Daniel was born into a royal family in the kingdom of Judah. But his silver spoon soon tarnished. As a young man he watched the army of Nebuchadnezzar march on Jerusalem. The city surrendered, and Nebu-chadnezzar demanded the collection of several royal hostages that he could take back to Babylon to guarantee the cooperation of this captured nation.

Daniel spent three years in Babylon learning the language, laws, and literature of the Babylonians. He graduated *summa cum laude*—top honors in his class! He then entered his career in government: a career that lasted over six decades. A career that saw numerous promotions and honors. A career that spanned the rule of at least four kings in two separate empires.

In six decades a politician can make many friends—and even more enemies. Enemies seething with jealousy, envy, anger, and resentment—emotions that gnaw at the insides of otherwise competent people and force them into irrational acts.

The crisis came near the end of Daniel's governmental career. The king appointed Daniel as one of the top three administrators over the government. (He had reached the level of senior cabinet minister.) But future promotions were on the horizon. "Daniel soon proved himself more capable than all the other administrators and princes. Because of his great ability, the king made plans to place him over the entire empire" (Daniel 6:3). Though in his eighties, Daniel was still leaving the competition in the dust!

How do you stop a politician in his tracks? Look for the dirt. Uncover the skeletons in the closet. Search out the smoking gun. Start with the premise that no one can be in public service very long without leaving a trail of incrimination. After all, no one is completely honest. "Then the other administrators and princes began searching for some fault in the way Daniel was handling his affairs" (6:4).

How well would you fare if a group of powerful individuals secretly decided to investigate you? They would spy on you at work. Record the time you arrive each morning and the time you leave every night.

Count the paper clips and pens in your drawer to see if so much as one is missing. Follow you home to see where you stop along the way. Look through your mail and magazines to see what you are reading. Rifle through your trash to see what you are eating. Monitor your television to see what you are watching. Check your tax returns for "irregularities" or unreported income. Look through your bank records to verify all deposits and checks. In short, what would your file look like if a group of enemies pulled out all the stops and spared no expense to uncover the real you?

Picture the scene in the darkened boardroom the night the private eyes presented their report on Daniel. Packed into the room that night were 120 satraps and the other two administrators. They came in vengeful glee, hoping to unmask Daniel and prove to themselves and to the king that Daniel was no better than the other rulers. The investigation had been long and arduous, made even more so by the need for secrecy. Neither Daniel nor the king could know of this private investigation. Had Daniel known, he might have been able to block the effort or take extra precautions to hide any incriminating evidence. Had the king known, he might have shown his displeasure at their petty jealousy by ordering their dismissal—or their death!

The room grew silent as the chief investigator stepped to the podium. With a grim frown on his face he announced to those gathered that "they couldn't find anything to criticize. He was faithful and honest and always responsible" (6:4). Daniel was squeaky clean!

The group of would-be antagonists reluctantly admitted two essential facts about Daniel's actions. First, they could find no evidence of corruption. Daniel had not taken bribes, skimmed money from the public treasury for private gain, received kickbacks, or provided political favors to friends. No sins of *commission* could be found.

Second, they could find no evidence of neglect. Daniel had not slacked off, cut corners, or ignored his responsibilities. He had faithfully done those things he was asked to do to the best of his ability. No sins of *omission* could be found.

No corruption. No neglect. Daniel was as honest as politicians come, and those gathered at this secret meeting had to be thinking the same thing that had been going through the king's mind: Daniel was in a league of his own.

A sharp tapping on the podium momentarily silenced the murmuring of the satraps. Don't abandon all hope, the speaker said as his face twisted into a sinister grin. Our search uncovered one other item. Though ignored at first, this one characteristic offered a ray of hope in an otherwise gloomy report. "Our only chance of finding grounds for accusing Daniel will be in connection with the requirements of his religion" (6:5).

Could there be a connection between Daniel's faith and his actions? Was Daniel such a straight arrow because of the heavenly Archer he served? To this group of disgruntled advisors, Daniel's one vulnerability was his unswerving devotion to his God. Daniel was so honest and consistent in his actions that an attack against his religious beliefs would not force him to change his routine.

Their plot was ingenious. Flatter the king by suggesting that all prayers for thirty days be directed only to him. Obviously the law was impractical and unenforceable, but that didn't matter. These leaders designed the law to entrap just one individual, and it worked to perfection. Daniel, Mr. Honest-As-They-Come, was not about to deny his God—or even hide his commitment to his God, for that matter. As soon as the king signed the law, the conspirators hurried to Daniel's house and found him praying by his open window "just as he had always done" (6:10).

Anyone can display godly character when the going is easy. Few steal if they are satisfied with what they possess. Few lie when speaking the truth is to their advantage. Few cheat on exams when they know all the answers. But character is formed in the midst of adversity.

The key to Daniel's success in surviving both the political investigation and the lions' den that followed was his honesty. After his miraculous deliverance, Daniel explained why he had been spared. "My God sent his angel to shut the lions' mouths so that they would not hurt me, for I have been found innocent in his sight. And I have not wronged you, Your Majesty" (6:22).

Where Has Honesty Gone?

Honesty is a character trait held in high regard throughout history. Millions of American schoolchildren grew up knowing the tale of George Washington confessing to his father, "I cannot tell a lie. I chopped down the cherry tree." Now, it is a bit disconcerting to find out that the story is untrue! Mason Weems, an American Episcopal clergyman who wrote a popular biography of George Washington entitled *The Life and Memorable Actions of George Washington,* invented the story. Somehow it seems ironic that a clergyman falsified a story about George Washington that was intended to teach honesty.

Though the story was not true, the lesson conveyed did influence another American some years later. Abraham Lincoln was born in Kentucky and grew up on the Indiana frontier. Formal education was the exception on the edge of civilization, but two books profoundly influenced Lincoln's life. The first was the Bible, and the second was Mason Weems's biography of George Washington. With these two books as his guide, is it any wonder that Abraham Lincoln became known as Honest Abe?

In just over a century, the Western world has moved from extolling the virtue of honesty to believing that honesty is not always the best policy. Don't get me wrong. I'm *not* saying that society was honest a century ago. Dishonesty has marred God's creation almost from the beginning. The first tempter, Satan, is called "a liar" (John

8:44). But the frequency of lying and the acceptability of lying are increasing at an alarming rate.

Gini Graham Scott identified one underlying cause of lying. "Basic insecurity causes people to lie. And the flip side is that secure, successful people don't need to lie."[3] In short, people lie because they are afraid that telling the truth will hurt them emotionally, socially, physically, or financially. But the sad truth is that, ultimately, being dishonest will cause far more suffering and inflict far more damage than being honest. Senator Gary Hart learned this truth in a very painful way.

After a distinguished career in the U. S. Senate, Gary Hart's bid for the 1988 Democratic presidential nomination was in high gear at the beginning of 1987. He was strongly favored in preliminary polls. Problems arose when rumors surfaced that he was a "womanizer." Senator Hart denied all allegations and challenged the media to prove the rumors. Some reporters accepted his challenge and began an investigation that resembled the one conducted against Daniel 2,500 years earlier. Unfortunately, the stakeout of Senator Hart's home did not find him praying in his upper window. When the *Miami Herald* reported on May 3, 1987, that Senator Hart had spent the evening with a woman who was not his wife, the senator denied the charge. But five days later he was forced to withdraw his bid for president when additional evidence surfaced that indicated the story was correct—and he was caught in a lie.

Later that year Senator Hart again entered the Democratic presidential primary. No single individual had taken a clear lead among the other candidates, and Senator Hart believed he had the vision that could unite the party and capture the interest of the voters. But his earlier popularity was gone. He had lost the trust of those who had once supported him. And trust is a fragile commodity. Once lost, it is extremely difficult to recover.

The Benefits of Honesty

In the back of our mind we all believe in the virtue of honesty. And yet, we all struggle with being dishonest. Well, actually, we don't like to think of it in those terms. We prefer to say we "fudge" a little on a report or test. We only tell "little white lies" so we won't hurt the feelings of others. And we "shade the truth" to enhance our popularity or fit in with the crowd. In effect, we lie to ourselves about our dishonesty with others.

But why should we tell the truth? What personal benefits will honesty bring? The Bible presents three specific, positive results of honesty. Honesty promotes trust, provides a positive role model for others, and pleases God.

HONESTY PROMOTES TRUST

Whom do you trust? Stop right now, and make a list of the five individuals you consider to be most trustworthy. They may be close friends, church or community leaders, radio or television personalities, national or international leaders. But the one common element must be that you trust them. Now look at your list and ask yourself what elements these individuals have in common. One specific item I'm sure they share is that you perceive them to be people who are honest. What they say, what they do with their money, how they perform at work, how they treat others—you trust those who have a reputation for honesty in these areas.

Now make a list of the five individuals you trust least. They can be neighbors, local or national leaders, religious or secular. Again, look at the list and ask yourself what elements these individuals share. Those you trust least are those you perceive to be dishonest. They have lied, cheated, or been dishonest in some way—and that's why you don't trust them.

God is trustworthy because he doesn't lie. Balaam was a "prophet for profit." He presented himself as a man who could bend the hand of God to do his bidding. The ancient king of Moab hired Balaam to put a curse on the people of Israel. But try as he might, Balaam could not force God's hand. Instead, God spoke to this pompous prophet through the mouth of a donkey. (Quite a put-down for someone claiming to be God's mouthpiece!) When Balaam finally opened his mouth before the king, his four messages came from God. And they showed that God could be trusted. "God is not a man, that he should lie. He is not a human, that he should change his mind. Has he ever spoken and failed to act? Has he ever promised and not carried it through?" (Numbers 23:19).

Why is God trustworthy? He doesn't lie, and he doesn't make empty promises. In short, he's honest. Period. We can stake our eternal destiny on God's promises. "Since we believe human testimony, surely we can believe the testimony that comes from God. And God has testified about his Son. . . . And this is what God has testified: He has given us eternal life, and this life is in his Son. So whoever has God's Son has life; whoever does not have his Son does not have life" (1 John 5:9, 11-12). God's honesty to us promotes trust in him. And that trust is essential for our eternal destiny.

Are you trustworthy? You like to think so. (You certainly *hope* others trust you!) But trust is a by-product of honesty. If you lie to others, no matter how small or insignificant the lie is, eventually you will be exposed. To the extent that you compromise your standards of honesty, you will lower the level of trust others have in you.

HONESTY PROVIDES A POSITIVE ROLE MODEL

The past few decades have seen a steep decline in honesty. Our post-Watergate society generally distrusts politicians, and what little trust remains is more deeply eroded with each election as candidates hurl charges and countercharges at each other. Political commercials blending half-truths and distorted facts promote one candidate by tearing down another. Even Honest Abe would have struggled under all the mud hurled by today's politicians.

Yet this is no time for Christians to give up. The truth of God's Word shines most brightly in the darkness. Our age does not have a monopoly on dishonesty. The same moral decline gripped the Roman Empire when the church was just beginning. Christians stood out because they displayed characteristics that were lacking in those around them.

The island of Crete epitomized the cesspool of moral values in the Roman world. In Greek literature "to Cretanize" was a euphemism for lying. In Titus 1:12 the apostle Paul quoted the Cretan poet Epimenides, who had described the moral state of his country five centuries earlier: "The people of Crete are all liars; they are cruel animals and lazy gluttons." Then Paul explained that the evaluation was still valid: "This is true" (1:13).

How could a society with a history of dishonesty ever change? The answer rested in the positive role models of those believers living in Crete. Paul spent the next chapter explaining how older men (2:2), older women (2:3), young women (2:4-5), young men (2:6-8), and even slaves (2:9-10) could become examples who could influence society. Titus was to "promote the kind of living that reflects right teaching" (2:1). Cretans may have been known the world over as liars, but the believers in Crete were to live by a different standard.

Passing new laws won't make society honest. There are not enough police today to enforce those laws already on the books. Technology won't make society honest. The Internal Revenue Service uses sophisticated computer programs to uncover tax fraud, but many still cheat on their income-tax returns. Stores spend billions of dollars on security, but shoplifting continues to increase.

The world needs examples of honesty in action. It needs role models of Christians who live out their faith in real life.

HONESTY PLEASES GOD

The bottom-line question on the issue of honesty is not how we feel about the issue but how God feels. What is God's view of honesty?

In Proverbs 11:1 Solomon wrote, "The Lord hates cheating, but he delights in honesty." In the original Hebrew the verse is quite colorful, capturing the necessity of honesty in daily life: "A false balance is an abomination to the Lord, but a just weight is his delight."

The marketplace buzzed with activity. Baskets of grain and jars of wine sat beside piles of grapes and figs just outside the city gate. Bargaining was brisk as the vendors hawked their wares. After agreeing on the price, the vendor would set up a pair of scales. The seller would place the appropriate weights on one side while the buyer placed some silver on the other. When the scales balanced, the payment was sufficient.

No bureaucracy existed to test and certify the scales of that day. Archaeologists have discovered stone weights at numerous sites, and no two sets of weights match exactly. The temptation for the seller to make each weight just a fraction heavier than the accepted standard was great. The average buyer would never know he or she had paid just slightly more than necessary during the transaction. But God knew. The point of Solomon's proverb is that *God* is the one who is pleased, or displeased, by such actions.

God expects honesty from those who claim him as their heavenly Father. He wants his children to share his "family likeness"—and that includes honesty. Yet some Christians use honesty as an excuse for being rude and obnoxious. Does being honest mean we must be offensive?

Speak the Truth in Love

In writing to the Ephesians, the apostle Paul spent the first half of his letter describing the spiritual wealth God had bestowed on his church. In the second half of the letter Paul focused on the "so what?" of each believer's new position. A believer's new position in Christ should produce practical changes in his or her day-to-day conduct. One of the first areas of change named by Paul is honesty. "So put away all falsehood and 'tell your neighbor the truth' because we belong to each other" (Ephesians 4:25).

I wonder what would have happened in the church at Ephesus had the leaders just read this one verse and then dismissed the congregation. Picture the scene on the way out as believers tried to apply this single verse.

Gaius: Good morning, Rufus! I didn't see you before the service began today. Say, has anyone been honest enough to tell you how hideous your new toga looks? It reminds me of something I would buy from a tent-maker rather than a seamstress. Of course, you have been gaining weight, so maybe it is best to try to hide everything.

Rufus: Why, thank you, Gaius! By the way, I've been meaning to tell you how obnoxious I find your wife and children. I don't know how you ever plan to marry off those two homely kids.

The toga may look terrible! And the children may be homely! But is this what Paul meant when he told the Ephesians to speak truthfully? No, it's not. Just a few verses earlier Paul focused on the motive that is to guide all speech. "We will hold to the truth *in love,* becoming more and more in every way like Christ" (4:15, italics added). Some things may be truthful, but they are best left unsaid if the one speaking is not motivated by love.

Honesty—guided by love—is always the best policy. Sometimes love requires us to hold our tongue rather than lash back in an unkind way. But at other times love requires us to tell our friends what they *need to hear,* even if the words are not what they *want to hear.* Such honesty will deepen most true friendships.

Solomon spoke of a friend's honesty in the book of Proverbs. True friends are those we trust to say the hard things—the rebukes that reveal blind spots in our lives. Solomon described the value of such honesty from friends.

- "Wounds from a friend are better than many kisses from an enemy." (Proverbs 27:6) A friend tells you what you need to hear, even if the truth hurts.
- "The heartfelt counsel of a friend is as sweet as perfume and incense." (27:9) Honest advice from a friend should make us thankful for his or her counsel.
- "As iron sharpens iron, a friend sharpens a friend." (27:17) A true friend sometimes causes friction

and sparks in our life, but the results are always positive.

Questions to Ponder

Most individuals today do not believe honesty is always the best policy. It can be uncomfortable, embarrassing, and unpopular—but God expects his children to share his passion for honesty.

1. In what areas of your life do you struggle with honesty?
2. What can you do in the next seven days to become more honest in your words and deeds?
3. Pray specifically for one individual this week, and ask God to use your honesty as a testimony to him or her of your faith in Christ.
4. Memorize Ephesians 4:15 and consciously try to "hold to the truth in love" in the coming days.

Listen to me! For I have excellent things to tell you. Everything I say is right, for I speak the truth and hate every kind of deception. (Proverbs 8:6-7)

2

COMPASSION

Do Nice Guys Finish Last?

Is Compassion out of Fashion?

Warning! Too much compassion may be hazardous to your health! That could have been the title of a humorous article in the *Dallas Morning News* some years back. The writer described the almost disastrous efforts of a kind librarian to help a stranded motorist.

> She was driving along and saw this man, standing beside his car, trying to flag somebody down. She stopped, and he said the battery was dead and asked if she'd mind giving him a shove to start his car.
>
> "Why, certainly," she said, "but I've never done this before."
>
> "Well, just get your speed up to about thirty, shove me along for a short distance and that should start it."
>
> "Are you sure?"
>
> "Certainly, I've done it a hundred times."

She backed up her car. Backed it up some more. And some more. Then she gunned the motor, burned rubber and came barreling like a missile toward the back of the man's car. He turned white as a ghost, screamed, prayed, jumped to the side of his car and started madly waving his arms. "No! Nooooo! Stop! Stoooopppp!" She mashed hard on the brakes, skidded, and managed to avoid a total disaster. "He did not," she said, "ever tell me I was supposed to put my bumper up against his first."[1]

We laugh at this story because it reminds us of situations in our lives where a lack of understanding caused problems. But the story has one sad twist. Most of us cannot fully relate to the librarian because we would *never* stop along the highway to help a stranger. Our fear of being robbed—or worse!—keeps us in our cars with our windows up and our doors locked. Compassion takes a backseat to fear.

But fear is not the fiercest foe of compassion. Selfishness is. The natural tendency is to look out for old number one—myself. We do not care for others because we are too absorbed with ourselves.

I grew up listening to the music of Peter, Paul, and Mary. I did not always agree with their political views, but I appreciated their candor. Time has grayed their hair, but it hasn't diminished their ability to focus on the state of society. In their twenty-fifth anniversary concert (a staple on PBS) Noel Paul Stookey delivered a monologue on our growing obsession with ourselves, and he did so by observing the ever diminishing focus of attention as represented in the titles of our most popular magazines.

In the 1950s the magazine of choice was *Life*. The name represented the breadth of interest in our society. We focused on all of life. Then in the 1960s another new magazine appeared: *People*. While it's true that people are a large part of life, they are not everything there is in life. In the 1970s another new magazine appeared, and the trend should have been obvious. The new magazine was *Us*. Stookey so humorously notes, "Now, 'us' is still people, too. Only it's not 'them,' it's only 'us.'" Then in the 1980s *Self* hit the newsstands. Stookey comments that any day he expects a new magazine called *Me*. All it will be is twenty pages of aluminum foil in which you can watch your reflection!

Yikes! Sometimes humor hurts. Perhaps unwittingly, the titles of new magazines stand as signposts that point in the direction society is heading. As we become more and more preoccupied with self, the attention we pay to others dwindles. Attitudes of callous indifference that once would have appalled us now produce little reaction.

Where Does the Me-First Philosophy Lead?

Susan Smith drove to the edge of John D. Long Lake in South Carolina. She stepped from the car and let it roll into the lake with her two sons strapped into their car seats. Though she knew her children were dead, she stuck by her story of being carjacked and publicly begged her "attacker" to return her children alive. When her crime finally became known, it shocked the nation. *Newsweek* reported, "Once again the perversity of human nature has confounded our expectations."[2] But Susan Smith is not the first to stifle her compassion for her children.

The prophet Jeremiah lived in times similar to our own. Society was crumbling. Values shifting. Compassion waning. Everything came crashing down when the armies of Babylon marched to the gates of Jerusalem. For over two years the Babylonians besieged Jerusalem. What remained of the moral fabric of society finally unraveled. Compassion gave way to a selfish desire to survive. "Survival of the fittest" became the watchword as the strong preyed on the weak. The first ones to go were the children. "Even the jackals feed their young, but not my people Israel. They ignore their children's cries, like the ostriches of the desert. The parched tongues of their little ones stick with thirst to the roofs of their mouths. The children cry for bread, but no one has any to give them" (Lamentations 4:3-4).

We react to Jeremiah's words with disbelief and horror. Yet our society borders on the same cynical, self-serving state. We reclassify the unborn child as a "fetus" or a "mass of tissue" to justify murder for the ease and convenience of our lifestyle. A pregnancy might be unwanted or unplanned, but either reason is still a selfish excuse for murder. Abortion is not the problem—it's merely a symptom.

Our materialistic society values

- things over people
- self-expression over submission
- personal pleasure over service to others
- acquiring over sharing
- results over relationships

It might be a dog-eat-dog world, but does that mean we must expect savage, self-serving behavior? Politicians rail against the lack of basic human values in society; one of the first casualties was compassion.

The Nation's "Terrible Twos"

The United States has barely passed through the celebration of its second century as a nation. Just out of diapers historically, it's a mere youngster among other world civilizations. If the United States were an actual child, perhaps we could attribute its present selfishness and violence to "the terrible twos"—that age when an apparently sweet child turns nasty.

The Bible presents a detailed account of another nation that struggled through its terrible twos. The nation was Israel. Just two centuries after entering God's Promised Land, Israel was out of control. Like the terrible two that it was, the nation crossed its arms and said no to God. Childish tantrums, foolish actions, and violent outbursts alternated with periods of relative peace and calm. A strong, active parent can help modify these childish outbursts, but that leader was absent in Israel. It was the time of the judges, when "Israel had no king, so the people did whatever seemed right in their own eyes" (Judges 17:6; 21:25).

A two-year-old without parental observation is a frightening thought. Picture your house or apartment being invaded by a curious, unsupervised two-year-old. I look up from my computer, and I see a set of Depression-era glasses sitting on a hutch shelf whispering, "Come and break me!" My daughter's open viola case rests on a couch immediately behind me. Just down the hall to my left sits a hot iron on the ironing board. The potential for material damage or physical harm is immense! The child needs supervision.

But how does a selfish nation produce a compassionate king? Where could Israel turn to find the kind of leader it needed in its time of desperation? God revealed the answer in the book of Ruth.

From Blessing to Barrenness

The historical background to the events recorded in the book of Ruth is given in 1:1—"in the days when the judges ruled." This was a period of national, religious, and moral decay, when foreign powers oppressed the people of Israel. The difficulties experienced by the nation during the period of the judges resulted from disobedience to God's law.

The period of the judges was a time when the people did not love the Lord with all their heart, soul, and mind. Nor did they "love your neighbor as yourself." These two commands summarize the terms of God's covenant with Israel. What Israel needed was a strong leader who would lead the people back to the covenant so they could experience God's blessings. The book of Ruth provides the thread that binds these themes together.

The way from barrenness to blessing comes by choosing God's covenant and walking in obedience to it. This is illustrated in the lives of Ruth ("Your people will be my people, and your God will be my God," 1:16) and Boaz ("But if he is not willing [to act as family redeemer], then as surely as the Lord lives I will," 3:13). It is no accident that a descendant of these two faithful individuals ultimately became Israel's king and reversed the barrenness of the period of the judges, bringing covenant faithfulness through the monarchy. The individual story of God's provision for Naomi through the faithfulness of Boaz and Ruth parallels the national story of God's provision for the nation through the descendant of Boaz and Ruth.

Naomi, her husband, and their two children crossed from Israel to Moab to pursue a better life. Refugees fleeing famine, they hoped to start over in this new country. Excitement turned to grief, however, when Naomi's husband suddenly died. Naomi, now a middle-aged woman with two older sons, saw her options dwindle. The marriages of the sons to foreign women probably caused a twinge of guilt, but the daughters-in-law proved to be wonderful wives who displayed great love for their husbands and their new mother-in-law.

Tragedy struck about ten years later when both sons died unexpectedly. Three grieving widows sat together lamenting their unbearable misfortune when word arrived that the famine in Israel had ended. A bitter, barren Naomi summoned the last of her resolve and decided it was time to return home.

Her faithful daughters-in-law obediently packed their belongings to join Naomi on her journey. Naomi released them from their obligation to her and urged them to return to their families. One turned back, but the other refused to go. "I will go wherever you go and live wherever you live. Your people will be my people, and your God will be my God" (1:16). Ruth cared for Naomi, and her compassion came from the truth she had learned about Naomi's God.

The journey from Moab to Bethlehem was brutal. The path that wound down the mountains of Moab ended on the tongue of land that cuts across the Dead Sea. Carrying everything they owned in small bundles slung over their backs, the two women waded through the water to the west side of the Dead Sea. The hot sun baked the land and sucked the water of the Dead Sea skyward.

En Gedi proved to be a welcome relief from the barren trek beside the Dead Sea. Here Naomi and Ruth would have washed the grime from their faces and filled their water skins with the clear, cool liquid from the "spring of the wild goats." But En Gedi also reminded them of the hard journey ahead. The path wound its way up the cliffs—climbing ever higher as the vegetation again gave way to the barrenness of the wilderness.

The long climb brought the exhausted women to the twisted landscape of the Judean wilderness. The path from En Gedi to Jerusalem snaked its way along the countless ravines, over ground strewn with flinty rock. Perhaps less than a week after they began their arduous journey from Moab, the two women walked wearily into Bethlehem.

Realistically, the situation looked grim for Naomi and Ruth. Both were widows, without husbands to protect or provide for them. They had no wealth, no resources, no prospects. The younger woman was a stranger who would face the stigma and prejudice of being a foreigner. No strong government existed to care for them. This was the time of the judges, remember. If two individuals ever needed compassion, Naomi and Ruth were the ones.

Along Comes Boaz

Striding across the opening verse of Ruth 2 is Boaz. Besides introducing him as a relative of Naomi's late husband, the writer also pictures him as "a wealthy and influential man" (2:1). In most Western countries today we associate that phrase with money, power, and prestige. And all of these are involved to some extent. Boaz did have enough wealth to control numerous fields, and he maintained control over those who worked for him. But Boaz's wealth and influence also involved his moral condition. He had a good reputation among the people. He was a man of integrity and character. He was a man of compassion. And this side of his personality played a key role in the remainder of the story. Boaz displayed four characteristics of compassion that set him apart from the other men of Bethlehem.

HE SPOKE KINDLY

Driven by a need to gather food for herself and her mother-in-law, Ruth made her way out to the fields of golden barley that surrounded Bethlehem like a patchwork quilt. God's law allowed her to follow the workers and pick up those pieces of grain they dropped. God had specifically told the Israelites, "When you harvest the crops of your land, do not harvest the grain along the edges of your fields, and do not pick up what the harvesters drop.

Leave it for the poor and the foreigners living among you" (Leviticus 23:22). Ruth, the poor foreigner, certainly qualified for this provision!

Boaz visited his fields to supervise the harvest. A social chasm separated Boaz from his laborers. He was the wealthy and influential man; they were the hired servants. He owned the fields; they worked in them. It's natural for tensions to exist between owners and workers, between the haves and the have-nots. But Boaz didn't look down on his servants.

As Boaz arrived at the fields being harvested, he greeted the harvesters. "The Lord be with you!" They responded in kind. "The Lord bless you!" (Ruth 2:4). Boaz's words reveal his kind spirit. He cared for his workers, and he was verbal in expressing his greeting and love. The workers' response hints of their appreciation for him. Boaz was a kind employer, and they respected him.

The power of kind words is amazing. Just ask Mrs. Driskoll's students. Julia Driskoll taught fifth grade at Scott Elementary School in Espy, Pennsylvania. Boys in fifth grade like baseball and bicycles. Recess is their favorite class. But Mrs. Driskoll had a kind spirit that made even subjects like geography, history, and math interesting and exciting.

I really don't remember much about school before fifth grade, but I remember Mrs. Driskoll's class. I will forever remember the location of the Carlsbad Caverns because I got to mold them in clay on our plaster-of-Paris-and-chicken-wire model of the southwestern United States. I discovered that learning can be fun because Mrs. Driskoll made it so. Her enthusiasm was contagious, and her compassion ran deep.

But the high point for her kind words had to be the spring operetta. Someone had decided the fifth-grade classes would produce a musical version of "The Frog Prince." Cardboard trees, a cardboard well, and cardboard castle walls stretched the artistic abilities of the various classes, and new layers of tempera paint found their way onto the walls of the art room. Somehow Mrs. Driskoll persuaded me to play the part of the frog prince (a dual role!). Everything went smoothly until dress rehearsal. Throughout most of the play I wore my frog costume, but in the final act I changed into the prince. Nobody ever told me the prince wore green leotards!

Asking a fifth-grade boy to wear leotards in a school play is roughly equivalent to asking an adult to stand naked in front of his or her peers. No way! Nope! Not a chance! The play was in jeopardy, and Julia Driskoll had to spring into action. To this day I don't remember what she said. But I remember her talking to me in the principal's office (it was the dressing room!). And I remember her kindness and concern for me. Somehow she talked me into those green leotards! The play went on as planned, and it received rave reviews from the parents of fifth graders who attended.

I've only had a handful of teachers like Julia Driskoll, but they have left an indelible mark on my life. I don't always remember what they said or the specific subjects they taught, but I remember their kindness and compassion. Boaz would have made an excellent fifth-grade teacher.

HE CARED DEEPLY

Words are an important way to express compassion, but words ring hollow if they are not accompanied by actions. Boaz could speak kindly because he was kindhearted. His care blazed most brightly when he spotted Ruth gleaning among his workers. When Boaz asked the foreman about Ruth, the foreman gave a succinct answer (Ruth 2:6-7):

- "She is the young woman from Moab" (She's a foreigner.)
- "Who came back with Naomi" (She's faithful to her mother-in-law.)
- "She asked me this morning if she could gather grain behind the harvesters" (She's respectful of authority.)
- "She has been hard at work ever since" (She's a dedicated worker.)

Boaz showed his care by providing for Ruth's protection and provision. A single woman, especially a foreigner, faced danger when she ventured alone into the fields. Boaz encouraged Ruth to stay with his reapers: "I have warned the young men not to bother you" (2:9). He also went out of his way to provide for her physical needs. "And when you are thirsty, help yourself to the water they have drawn from the well" (2:9). Boaz followed his words of kindness with specific actions.

HE ACCEPTED WARMLY

Some might think Boaz was attracted to Ruth only because of her beauty, but the text suggests otherwise. Boaz was impressed by her faithfulness and devotion to her mother-in-law and by her hard work. After his kind protection Ruth stood in amazement. "'Why are you being so kind to me?' she asked. 'I am only a foreigner'" (Ruth 2:10). Ruth realized that not all Israelites appreciated her presence. Though she had been in town only a short time, she may already have heard the verbal slurs and seen the little signs of hostility that said, You're not one of us! Why was Boaz so different?

Boaz's answer spoke volumes. "'Yes, I know,' Boaz replied. 'But I also know about the love and kindness you have shown your mother-in-law'" (2:11). When Boaz looked at Ruth he did not see a Moabitess. Instead, he saw a daughter-in-law who cared so deeply for her mother-in-law that she was willing to risk racial slurs and personal attacks to provide the food her mother-in-law needed.

Boaz saw Ruth through the eyes of God. And he wished for God's blessing to be on this kindhearted foreigner. "May the Lord, the God of Israel, under whose wings you have come to take refuge, reward you fully" (2:12).

Some in Bethlehem may have barely tolerated the presence of this foreigner in their midst. Perhaps they resented her because of earlier battles between Moab and Israel. Certainly many Israelites lost their lives when Eglon, king of Moab, oppressed Israel for eighteen years (Judges 3:12-14). Perhaps they begrudged her the pieces of grain she took from the fields—grain they may have coveted for themselves. But Boaz was different. He saw her faithfulness and hoped the Lord would bless her. Little did he know that God would fulfill his wish—through him!

Ruth was appreciative. Though socially she was even a lower-class citizen than his workers, Boaz displayed acceptance. That Boaz had comforted her and spoken kindly to her—two basic acts of compassion often in short supply—overwhelmed Ruth.

HE ACTED GENEROUSLY

Boaz had kind intentions, but his compassion was also practical. Words of comfort are nothing more than idle wishes unless they are accompanied by generous deeds. We have all known individuals who know all the right words but who never move their intentions from their mouth to their hands.

At midday the heat in Bethlehem was most oppressive. The sun shone directly overhead from a cloudless sky. Its intensity sapped the strength of those who had been at work since sunup. The workers drifted to the protection of the temporary booths set up beside the fields. Here clay pots held water while fresh-roasted grain and bread provided nourishment for the weary workers. The hired laborers expected such arrangements, but the owner had no obligation to provide for those who were not in his employment.

Ruth had no illusions of receiving special favors the morning she first went to the harvest fields. Her greatest hope was that no one would harass her. Boaz's earlier words of kindness had taken her by surprise, but at noon he approached her and said, "Come over here and help yourself to some of our food. You can dip your bread in the wine if you like." As Ruth stepped into the shade of the booth with the other workers, "Boaz gave her food—more than she could eat" (Ruth 2:14).

Boaz's generosity must have amazed Ruth. Boaz was not stingy with his words of praise—or his food!

Boaz met Ruth's immediate needs for food, rest, and shelter. But his generosity extended beyond those specific acts of visible kindness. As she left, he turned to his men and ordered them to be inefficient harvesters for Ruth's sake! "Let her gather grain right among the sheaves without stopping her. And pull out some heads of barley from the bundles and drop them on purpose for her. Let her pick them up, and don't give her a hard time!" (2:15-16). Boaz provided for Ruth's long-term needs, and he did so in a way that protected her dignity.

After just one day, Naomi knew God was at work. When Ruth returned from the harvest, she carried over half a bushel of grain. That was far more than one would expect from a single worker picking up stray pieces of grain that had fallen from the workers' hands. No wonder Naomi asked, "Where did you gather all this grain today? Where did you work? May the Lord bless the one who helped you!" (2:19).

Boaz's generosity extended throughout the barley and wheat harvest. For nearly two months Ruth worked alongside Boaz's laborers. She found protection, acceptance, and encouragement. In short, she found compassion.

The Results of Compassion

One man's compassion made the difference in the lives of two widowed women—Ruth and Naomi. The story provides a bright spot in an otherwise dark chapter in Israel's history. While everyone else was doing "whatever seemed right in their own eyes," Boaz did what was right in God's eyes. But what difference could such an act of kindness make nationally? Could the compassion of one man in one small town influence the entire nation? The final chapter of the book of Ruth says yes!

As in a charming fairy tale, Ruth and Boaz overcame adversity and got married. But instead of picturing the couple living happily ever after, the writer ends by sharing the legacy the couple left that extended far beyond their days in Israel. Ruth and Boaz had a son named Obed. That child grew up and had a son named Jesse. He grew up and had eight sons—the youngest of whom was King David! The compassion of Ruth for Naomi and the compassion of Boaz for Ruth ultimately produced Israel's greatest king. The book that begins "in the days when the judges ruled" (Ruth 1:1) ends with David, the king who set the nation aright. The pivotal link in the transition from chaos to the kingdom is the book of Ruth—and the compassion of Ruth and Boaz!

Hesed Projects

I first joined the faculty of Dallas Theological Seminary in 1981. In the early years of my teaching, I was very academic in my approach. I had midterm and final exams because I wanted my students to memorize key Bible facts. But one summer, my perspective changed completely.

I was teaching my favorite class, a survey of the prophets, in a five-week summer session. I had midterm and final exams already prepared. Everything was ready, and I was excited (perhaps even a bit proud). My students would come away understanding each of the Old Testament prophets.

But something went radically wrong that summer. During the five-week period when I was teaching that course, three individuals whom I had known while a student at seminary failed morally. Each destroyed his family, damaged a ministry, and brought disrespect to the name of Christ. How could that happen? We had sat through the same seminary classes, studied the same Bible, taken the same tests. Yet the truth of God's Word somehow had not penetrated their hearts. Something was wrong!

That traumatic summer changed my approach to teaching. As I prayed through what I could do to help other students avoid those pitfalls, I concluded that merely memorizing facts is not enough. Unless we work to apply it to our lives, we can become hardened to God's Word. We can grow cold in our relationship with others unless we work hard to develop compassion, concern, and care.

Today I have replaced my midterm and final exams with "*hesed* projects." I tell my students these are the most important projects they will have to do all year. They must complete two such projects to pass my course. But what is a *hesed* project? Let me quote from my class syllabus.

Hesed is the Old Testament word for "loyalty love" that has the implied idea of loving faithfulness to a covenant relationship. The Old Testament wisdom literature and prophets continually stress the need for covenant faithfulness—both to God and to man. One danger in seminary is the tendency to become "hearers of the Word only"—to divorce knowledge from response. Believers must take time to cultivate and maintain covenant faithfulness in their relationships with others. These two *hesed* projects are given in place of midterm and final exams to give each student an opportunity to find time to develop "loyalty love" with others.

Each "project" includes the following elements:
1. Plan an activity that you and someone else can do that will
   a. last about four hours
   b. not involve Seminary
   c. be a time of Christian fellowship and enjoyment
2. Participate in the activity.
3. Write a summary, and turn it in on the midterm and final reports.

Be creative in planning projects. If you are married, you might want to go on a picnic, go to the zoo, visit Fort Worth, bike around White Rock Lake, or visit some other place in Dallas that you have never seen. Remember, the emphasis should be on doing something the whole family can enjoy. If you are single, you can take your fiancée, or girl/boyfriend, or someone you want to befriend, and plan an activity for them. Take them to dinner (or cook a "gourmet" meal for them), go on a hike together, go fishing, take them to a sporting event, etc. Take time to enjoy the fellowship of another's company.

The response over the past decade has been overwhelming. I have a file of cards, letters, and hand-drawn pictures from the spouses and children of students thanking me for the *hesed*-project assignment. I receive calls from former students who tell me they still have family hesed projects.

Loyalty love and compassion fit together. Someone committed to a relationship will demonstrate care and compassion to the other individual. In Lamentations 3, Jeremiah found God's loyalty love and compassion, or mercy, to be twin pillars of hope. "The unfailing love *[hesed]* of the Lord never ends! By his mercies we have been kept from complete destruction" (Lamentations 3:22). Just ten verses later, the prophet returns to these beacons of hope. "Though he brings grief, he also shows compassion according to the greatness of his unfailing love" (3:32). How deep is your reservoir of compassion?

Questions to Ponder

Think of someone on the forefront of business or politics, and you usually envision someone who is hard driving, tough, aggressive. But an individual on the vanguard of the Christian life is a man or woman of compassion. Take some time to focus on several practical questions related to compassion.

1. Do you find it difficult to show compassion to some individuals?
2. If so, why do you find it so difficult to show care and compassion for them?
3. Choose one individual, and try to get to know that person better this week. Ask God for one specific opportunity to show compassion to that person.
4. Memorize Lamentations 3:22, and ask God to remind you of the compassion he has shown to you.

Is there any encouragement from belonging to Christ? Any comfort from his love? Any fellowship together in the Spirit? Are your hearts tender and sympathetic? Then make me truly happy by agreeing wholeheartedly with each other, loving one another, and working together with one heart and purpose. (Philippians 2:1-2)

3

WISDOM

Are You Some Kind of Wise Guy?

Knowledge or Wisdom?

All right, I confess. I'm a "Far Side" fan. My office has two "Far Side" calendars—one on my desk and one in my computer. We own all the "Far Side" books, along with a collection of shirts and mugs. My wife tolerates my passion for the perverse, and I think my son has inherited my love of the bizarre. I have struggled with withdrawal symptoms since Gary Larson stopped producing the piece.

One of my favorite "Far Side" comics shows the outside steps leading up to Midvale School for the Gifted. At the top of the steps stands one of these gifted students, books cradled in his right hand, with his left hand vainly pushing against the outside door to open it. Just above the student is a sign on the door that says (in very *large* letters) PULL.

That particular comic speaks to me because it distinguishes between knowledge and wisdom. The students attending the school in Larson's comic were expected to have a high level of knowledge. That doesn't guarantee that they are wise.

The buzzwords for the twenty-first century are *Internet, information superhighway,* and *World Wide Web.* Instant access to a world of information is the technological millennium some are seeking. The assumption seems to be that availability of information will lead to wisdom.

But you cannot equate information with wisdom. There is a large chasm between the availability of information and the acquiring of wisdom. Data and information (not all of it accurate) abound in our society. But most individuals still make poor choices in how they live their lives.

The Hebrews understood the difference between knowledge and wisdom. Their word for wisdom *(hokmah)* carried with it the idea of skill. Wisdom was the ability to live life skillfully and successfully. Knowledge alone does not guarantee that life will be lived skillfully.

About five years ago I took up golf. I have reached the point in my game where I'm awful—and that's an improvement over where I began! I understand the fundamentals of golf. I've studied golf magazines, read golf books, and watched golf videos. Approaching the game as an academician enabled me to master the essential facts.

As I play through a round of golf in my head, I can score in the upper seventies or low eighties. Unfortunately, a round of golf must also be played on the golf course. And as Shakespeare said through Hamlet, "Ay, there's the rub!" My brain can score in the upper seventies, but my body struggles to break a hundred! I know the information, but

I do not yet have the skill to put the information to use successfully.

Society is drowning in a sea of information—but people can still make very foolish choices. We know the effects of smoking, excessive drinking, and drugs; but all three still entice and enslave otherwise intelligent people.

A small flaw can cause great difficulty. In April 1990 the space shuttle *Discovery* launched the 1.5 billion-dollar Hubble Space Telescope into orbit. The telescope was a masterpiece of engineering—but one flaw nearly undid the entire project. One mirror was incorrectly made, and its surface, though only slightly flawed, blurred the images from the telescope. Three years later, a separate shuttle mission performed a series of delicate repairs on the telescope to correct the flaw. The new optics served as "cosmic glasses" to correct the telescope's celestial nearsightedness. The flaw seemed small, but it took years of effort and hundreds of millions of dollars to correct.

When some small problem threatens to undo an otherwise good thing, we describe it as "a fly in the ointment." That phrase originally came from the pen of the wisest of Israel's kings—Solomon. He had a knack for turning a phrase, and the whole proverb goes, "Dead flies will cause even a bottle of perfume to stink! Yes, an ounce of foolishness can outweigh a pound of wisdom and honor" (Ecclesiastes 10:1). The phrase teaches us much about wisdom and folly—and about Solomon. To understand the full meaning of Solomon's words we need to sit down, take out the family album, and study three snapshots of Solomon taken at different times in his life.

Snapshot #1: Young Solomon Asking for Wisdom

"King David is dead! Long live King Solomon!" The words swirled through Jerusalem's dusty streets and echoed off the stone walls of this fortress-city. David lived his life in epic proportions, both in his triumphs and in his tragedies. The shadow of Israel's greatest warrior and king threatened to obscure his young heir to the throne. Following a legend is tough.

David's unwise marriages to multiple wives, compounded by his adultery with Bathsheba, produced a chaotic and fractured home. One son raped his half sister and was, in turn, murdered by his half brother (2 Samuel 13). One son led a civil war against King David and received support from a relative of Bathsheba (chapter 15). At the end of David's life one son plotted to succeed him as king, only to be thwarted when David appointed Solomon (1 Kings 1). Had they lived back then, Oprah, Sally, and Geraldo would have clamored to put David's family on their shows!

Now young Solomon sits uneasily on his father's throne. His father's last words of advice were whispered warnings about Joab, the former commander of Israel's army who had betrayed David and plotted to put Solomon's brother on the throne. Solomon's first act as king was to foil still another plot to take his throne and to give orders to execute the two conspirators—his brother and Joab (chapter 2). What had he gotten himself into?!

The burden of following in the footsteps of his illustrious father, reigning wisely as king and knowing how to discern between right and wrong, gnawed at the young king. Anyone ever thrust into a place of leadership and responsibility knows the sense of inadequacy that must have gripped Solomon. He was now responsible for making life-and-death decisions. Things that had seemed so clear to him as he stood on the periphery now seemed complex and involved as he tried to explore all sides to make fair and impartial judgments.

Two dangers face an individual in a position of power and authority. One danger is that the leader will become paralyzed by the enormity of the task. The leader is responsible for others, and a single mistake or miscalculation can cost those followers their jobs, their families, or their lives.

Most decisions are not black and white. The leader must sort through conflicting reports, incomplete data, and divided supporters to decide what is best. A leader can become so afraid of making a mistake that he or she will analyze—and reanalyze—every possible angle and option and do nothing unless one option emerges as the clear choice. Some call this paralysis by analysis.

The second danger is that the leader will become self-centered and prideful. Position brings with it prestige and perks, and a leader can become sidetracked by these trappings of power. Most corrupt politicians do not enter politics with evil motives. They begin with a genuine desire to make a difference for others. But the constant pressures and demands of those who seek their attention or their help desensitize them. A leader can then justify receiving gifts from supporters seeking access to those in power, accepting financial rewards for political favors, or even taking kickbacks from those who receive government contracts.

Alone. Vulnerable. Uncertain. Unsure how to proceed. Solomon must have doubted his father's wisdom in making him king. He was *not* the warrior his father had been. But he had inherited his father's desire to follow God. And so it's no surprise that our first snapshot of Solomon finds him kneeling before God in Gibeon asking for God's wisdom in his hour of need.

Solomon traveled nearly eight miles northwest from Jerusalem to Gibeon to seek the Lord because God's temple in Jerusalem was still nothing more than a dream passed on from David to his son. Four years would pass before Solomon could begin the project. So Solomon traveled to Gibeon to worship at the most important altar in Israel (3:4). What made it so important? "At that time, the Tabernacle of the Lord and the altar that Moses made in the wilderness were located at the hill of Gibeon" (1 Chronicles 21:29).

Solomon made a pilgrimage to the tent of God built by Moses himself. He stood before the altar first consecrated by Moses 476 years earlier and offered sacrifices to the living God. Perhaps Solomon looked for strength in his spiritual heritage. Perhaps he felt so inadequate that he longed for a visible sign of God's blessing. Whatever his motivation, his willingness to offer a thousand burnt offerings on the altar demonstrated his dedication to God and his dependence on God for the task ahead.

Many leaders struggle with a crushing sense of their own inadequacy. Their followers put them on pedestals and assume they see all, hear all, know all, and can do all. But true leaders know better. They see beyond the hype and hoopla to understand their limitations and inadequacies. Solomon came to God because he was acutely aware of his need for God's help.

The Lord responded to Solomon's act of worship and devotion. Appearing to him at night, God made the ultimate offer. "What do you want? Ask, and I will give it to you!" (1 Kings 3:5). God offered Solomon the chance of a lifetime!

A persistent childhood fantasy is the desire to have all our wishes fulfilled. Our childhood desire to own Aladdin's lamp might be replaced with the hope of winning the Publisher's Clearing House sweepstakes—or the state lottery. But be honest: The thought of "having it all" appeals to us all.

What's amazing about this first snapshot of Solomon is how he responded to God's offer. Foremost in his mind was his need for wisdom, not wealth. "O Lord my God, now you have made me king instead of my father, David, but I am like a little child who doesn't know his way around" (3:7). Solomon sensed his inexperience and inadequacy.

What should he ask for? Money? Security? Protection? Long life? Solomon's answer was profound in its simplicity and honesty. "Give me an understanding mind so that I can govern your people well and know the difference between right and wrong. For who by himself is able to govern this great nation of yours?" (3:9). Solomon asked God for wisdom to do what was right in leading the people of Israel.

God rewarded Solomon for his humble request. "The Lord was pleased with Solomon's reply and was glad that he had asked for wisdom" (3:10). Solomon put his responsibility to Israel ahead of any desire for personal reward. God not only gave Solomon the "wise and understanding mind" he requested (3:12), God also rewarded Solomon with "riches and honor" (3:13). God promised Solomon he would be wise—and wealthy!

So how did Solomon do? The writer of 1 Kings includes five incidents that reveal the extent of the wisdom God gave Solomon.

WISDOM TO ADMINISTER JUSTICE

The first test for Solomon's wisdom was not long in coming. Two prostitutes came before the king, each claiming custody of a newborn baby boy. Both women had given birth to sons, but one child had died. Each woman claimed the dead child belonged to the other while she was the legitimate parent of the child who remained alive.

The child still alive was but a baby—too young to help in establishing identity. No witnesses were available to vouch for either woman. Each story was plausible, and each woman was passionate in arguing her side. How could Solomon administer justice when the truth could not be established beyond a reasonable doubt?

Solomon revealed his God-given wisdom in his response to the women. His initial decision to slice the living child in half and divide him between the women revealed the compassion of the true mother. Solomon awarded the child to the rightful woman. He looked beyond the obvious to establish justice—and his wisdom made an impression on others. "Word of the king's decision spread quickly throughout all Israel, and the people were awed as they realized the great wisdom God had given him to render decisions with justice" (1 Kings 3:28).

One little postscript. I remember hearing this story as a young boy in Sunday school. The fine points of the story were lost on me, but I walked home from church with a vivid picture of a king in purple robes and a crown holding a child's ankle in his left hand while raising a sword in his right to slice the boy in two. A few months later I put the story to use. Our next-door neighbor had four girls. I was playing in my backyard when I overheard two of the younger girls arguing over a Barbie doll. Each was trying to wrestle control of the doll away from the other as they shouted, "It's mine!" "No, it's mine!" Very Solomon-like I walked over, grabbed the doll, and offered to break it in half and give each sister a piece. When one screamed, "No!" I handed her the doll and told her it was hers. I felt very smug until the other sister went home to tell her mom that her sister and I were picking on her! Oh well, it worked for Solomon.

WISDOM TO ORGANIZE EFFICIENTLY

David built Israel into a great empire, but Solomon organized it to operate smoothly. He developed a central government and divided Israel into twelve districts, each with a district governor (1 Kings 4:1-19). Solomon also ruled over the surrounding nations captured by David. Evidently Solomon ruled these lands well, because the writer of Kings notes that "there was peace throughout the entire land" (4:24). Solomon's organization brought with it a time of security and prosperity unknown in the land of Israel up to that day. From "Dan to Beersheba"—from north to south in the land—the people "lived in peace and safety," and "each family had its own home and garden" (4:25).

WISDOM TO UNDERSTAND LIFE

Solomon was more than just a smart politician. He was a card-carrying member of Mensa before Mensa ever existed! "His wisdom exceeded that of all the wise men of the East and the wise men of Egypt" (1 Kings 4:30). The writer singles out Solomon's accomplishments in literature (3,000 proverbs), music (1,005 songs), botany (all plants from the great cedar of Lebanon to the common hyssop), and zoology (animals, birds, reptiles, and fish). Solomon observed life at all levels, and his keen powers of observation and analysis helped him synthesize that knowledge.

WISDOM TO KEEP PEACE

King David had many enemies during his lifetime, but he also made some powerful allies. One of these was King Hiram of Tyre. Solomon sent Hiram a letter reaffirming his friendship and proposing a business deal. If Hiram would supply cedarwood for the temple, Solomon would pay Hiram and the laborers for the work. Solomon was quick to compliment Hiram on his skilled workers. "As you know, there is no one among us who can cut timber like you Sidonians!" (1 Kings 5:6). Hiram agreed, and their relationship prospered. Such cooperation was no accident. "The Lord gave great wisdom to Solomon just as he had promised. And Hiram and Solomon made a formal alliance of peace" (5:12).

WISDOM TO EXALT GOD

Throughout these early years, Solomon never forgot the source of his wisdom and great ability. His father had wanted to build a temple for God in Jerusalem, but God had not permitted David to do so. Now, however, Solomon dedicated himself to that task. For seven years Solomon devoted his energy, insight, and accumulated wealth to the building of a house for God. But Solomon did not let his religious devotion crowd out God. "Even the highest heavens cannot contain you. How much less this Temple I have built!" (1 Kings 8:27). Later in life Solomon encapsulated the essence of wisdom and knowledge—and said it began with a proper relationship to God. "Fear of the Lord is the beginning of knowledge. Only fools despise wisdom and discipline" (Proverbs 1:7).

Our first snapshot of Solomon is impressive. We see a man with a proper understanding of his limited abilities and God's unbounded grace. In seeking God's wisdom, Solomon found the key that unlocked his full potential as a leader. And that wisdom helped Solomon in all areas of life—from affairs of state, to observations on life, to worship.

Snapshot #2: Wayward Solomon Pursuing Wives

The original snapshot, perhaps slightly dog-eared, was now just a memory in Solomon's photo album of life.

Solomon had gazed at the picture frequently during his early days as king, but new interests entered his life to crowd out old commitments. Somewhere in the busyness of life, Solomon made a wrong turn. The wisest of men was undone by a foolish mistake—one so subtle as to elude even the champion of observation.

A new snapshot shows Solomon entering a period that pundits today would describe as his midlife crisis. At first glance the photo looks as if it were taken at a large family reunion or gathering. Individual faces are hard to recognize because the photographer had to stand at a distance to get everyone in the picture. A thousand women, countless children, and one distracted man pause in their pursuit of pleasure to have their activities immortalized on this verbal snapshot of life in the royal court. What went wrong?

A careful look at this second snapshot reveals three reasons why the wisest of men made so many foolish mistakes. Solomon allowed three tiny cracks to appear in the foundation of his life, and those cracks widened to bring his godly life crashing down. Study the snapshot carefully—and learn from Solomon's mistakes.

SOLOMON PURSUED FORBIDDEN PLEASURE

Power and prestige attract individuals who hope to profit from such connections. No doubt merchants and business-men crowded into Solomon's palace every day, seeking to secure the king's blessing—and financial backing—for building projects, trading partnerships, and other ventures. The court had a cosmopolitan flair as dignitaries and envoys from countless nations around Israel sought an audience with the king to cement trade agreements and treaties.

One way to ratify a treaty between two nations was through marriage. A king would give his daughter (or another young woman from the royal family) in marriage to the king of another nation. Many of Solomon's marriages were likely the result of such arrangements. Evidently Solomon's Achilles' heel was his love of pleasure—especially the pleasure of beautiful women. It probably did not take long for these envoys to realize that a good way to seal an agreement with Solomon was to give him a lovely young woman in marriage as part of the bargain.

The Bible doesn't mince words about Solomon's weakness. "Now King Solomon loved many foreign women. . . . He had seven hundred wives and three hundred concubines. And sure enough, they led his heart away from the Lord" (1 Kings 11:1, 3).

Solomon lived life full throttle, and he had the resources to support his craving for good things. In the book of Ecclesiastes Solomon confesses, "Anything I wanted, I took. I did not restrain myself from any joy" (2:10).

Pleasure itself is not wrong, but it can turn one's eyes away from the Lord. Solomon became more intent on gratifying himself than on pleasing God. The first tiny crack appeared in the foundation of his life, and it grew in proportion to the size of Solomon's harem.

SOLOMON IGNORED GOD'S WORD
God didn't intend for us to live our lives in misery! But in pursuing pleasure one must remain within the bounds of

God's Word. On two key points Solomon chose to ignore specific prohibitions found in God's Word—and his disobedience in these two areas produced the second crack in his foundation.

In 1 Kings 11 the author sadly records Solomon's marriages to women from the nations around Israel. "The Lord had clearly instructed his people not to intermarry with those nations, because the women they married would lead them to worship their gods. Yet Solomon insisted on loving them anyway" (11:2).

Perhaps Solomon struggled when the first of these foreign women arrived with the envoy from a neighboring state. As the envoy fawned over Solomon and described the mutual benefits of the proposed treaty for Solomon and the people of Israel, Solomon barely listened. Instead, his eyes kept moving back to take in the form and beauty of this remarkable woman who stood in his royal court. Surely God wasn't referring to *this* woman when he made such a prohibition against having foreign wives, or else why would God have made her so beautiful?

No doubt Solomon used his great intellect to construct several rationalizations for why God would consider this marriage to be an exception. But in the end Solomon deliberately decided to disobey God's Word and follow the lust of his heart.

Somewhat later in life Solomon came to a sad realization. "All people spend their lives scratching for food, but they never seem to have enough" (Ecclesiastes 6:7). Solomon had an appetite for beautiful women, and his appetite was never satisfied. In Deuteronomy 17:17 God had commanded Israel's future kings to guard their hearts. "The king must not take many wives for himself, because they will lead him away from the Lord." Solomon must have known this command, but as each new woman arrived in his royal court, he rationalized that just one more wife wouldn't make a great difference. (After all, God had not set a specific number, had he?) I wonder how long Solomon lived before he woke up one day and realized he had accumulated one thousand wives and concubines.

SOLOMON ALLOWED HIS LOVE FOR GOD TO GROW COLD

Solomon's pursuit of pleasure and his benign neglect of God's Word caused a subtle transformation in his own life. This crack in his moral foundation was the most insidious because it happened so slowly that he never saw the change until it was too late. But over time his love for God grew cold, and his heart grew callous. "In Solomon's old age, [his wives and concubines] turned his heart to worship their gods instead of trusting only in the Lord his God, as his father, David, had done" (1 Kings 11:4).

Solomon began his reign by following the Lord, but his heart had become dulled by success. He started well, but he finished poorly. Part of living wisely is realizing that temptations can take different forms as we grow older. The crucible of conflict that brings us closer to God in our youth often becomes only a dim memory later in life. Our wealth multiplies, our reputation becomes established, our circle of friends increases—and the temptation to rely on ourselves instead of God grows. Recognizing the pleasures that allure us, remaining obedient to God's Word, and maintaining a warm relationship with the Lord are three wise actions that will help keep us faithful to God as we grow older. Solomon neglected all three—and he awoke one day to find that the wise young king had become a foolish old man.

Snapshot #3: Old Solomon Explaining the World

Sitting in front of a fire to ward off the numbing chill of Jerusalem's winter, Israel's aging monarch showed once again that though his body had grown old, his mind was still nimble. Staring out a window at nothing in particular, he mentally flipped through the pages of his life.

Solomon's photo album of life was nearly full. The more recent pages contained dark, shadowy images that were a sharp contrast to the brightness so evident in the earlier ones. How could a life that started with so much promise end in such despair? This is the mystery of life we want Solomon to explain.

His opening words rattle us. "Everything is meaningless . . . utterly meaningless!" (Ecclesiastes 1:2). The man of unparalleled intellect had set out to understand the meaning of life as we know it—and his conclusion was that life by itself is empty and hollow. Like a soap bubble that glistens in the sun, life appears to have substance and meaning until you try to grasp it. The second you get your hand around it, it disappears and leaves you empty.

Is this the cynical whining of a bitter old man? Or are Solomon's observations profound words of wisdom that can help us live wisely today? Many have assumed the former is true, but Solomon argues for the latter. The book of Ecclesiastes is Solomon's final photograph in his album of life, and it's a photographic masterpiece that captures the essence of life itself.

Solomon has no need to gloss over his failures in life. The self-photographs of Solomon's life in Ecclesiastes show every wart and wrinkle. Solomon's original God-given wisdom combines with the insight he gained from life's school of hard knocks. The result is an unretouched photograph of life as it really is.

Been There. Done That.
Solomon began his portrait by recounting everything he had done to find meaning in life as it's lived here on earth. The list is impressive.

GET A GOOD EDUCATION!
Solomon began his reign as a mental Superman, with powers far beyond those of mortal man. It was just natural that the first item on his to-do list was to figure out (using his fantastic powers of wisdom and observation) how life worked. "I devoted myself to search for understanding and to explore by wisdom everything being done in the world" (Ecclesiastes 1:13). Big mistake! The more he learned, the more he realized the futility of his ultimate goal. It was, he concluded, "like chasing the wind" (1:14).

In the thousands of years since Solomon, millions of individuals have devoted their lives to advancing knowledge. The more we know, the more we realize no one person can possibly understand how all life works. Scientists push the outer limits of knowledge by concentrating on ever smaller fields of specialization. This is the only way they can possibly learn all the knowledge available that is relevant to their research. As someone wryly observed, "We know more and more about less and less, until soon we will know everything about nothing." Only God can know everything about everything. Though education is helpful, no one person will ever gain enough knowledge to understand all of life. To think we can is futility.

GO FOR THE GUSTO!

Solomon didn't take long to switch his focus. If education can't supply the meaning of life, perhaps we can discover life's true meaning in the pursuit of pleasure. You only go around once in life, and you've got to grab for all the gusto you can get! may have become Solomon's motto at this point. His experiments ran the gamut: pleasure and laughter, mood-altering drugs, material possessions, wealth, sex, and personal influence (Ecclesiastes 2:1-9). Then he stopped to evaluate everything he had tried. His conclusion: "It was all so meaningless. It was like chasing the wind. There was nothing really worthwhile anywhere" (2:11).

Modern society perpetuates the myth that the essence of life is found in the pursuit of pleasure. Solomon reached the point where he "had it all," only to discover that it wasn't enough to bring meaning and purpose to life. Most today are not wise enough to know they are running down a dead-end street.

One of the most popular comic strips of the past few years (until he stopped drawing it!) was "Calvin and

Hobbes" by Bill Watterson. (More of his comics ended up taped to the front of our refrigerator than any other!) One of the most insightful—and funny—appeared on Saturday, May 27, 1995. In the first of four panels Calvin is walking across a fallen tree while his tiger friend, Hobbes, follows behind. Calvin says decisively, "Getting is better than having." In the next panel he turns to his friend to explain. "When you *get* something, it's new and exciting. When you *have* something, you take it for granted and it's boring." In the third panel Hobbes raises an objection: "But everything you *get* turns into something you *have.*" Calvin responds, "That's why you always need to get new things." The final panel ends with Hobbes waving his hand in front of himself while saying, "I feel like I'm in some stockholder's dream." Calvin gets in the last words by summarizing his philosophy: "'Waste and want,' that's *my* motto."

Too many today look for happiness in a new car (until it gets scratched!), a new dress (until someone else wears the same one to your party!), a new house (until the mortgage payments come due!), a new relationship (until it, too, turns sour), a new . . . The list is endless. Solomon tried it all—and discovered that "things" couldn't bring permanent satisfaction or give meaning to life.

WORK HARD!

Solomon's third attempt to find meaning in life took a more biblical approach. One purpose God assigned humanity was to exercise dominion over creation, and this included physical activity. God put Adam and Eve "in the Garden of Eden to tend and care for it" (Genesis 2:15). Perhaps the real meaning in life, Solomon reasoned, came through good, old-fashioned, hard work. Like many today, Solomon looked for life's meaning in his work.

But Solomon's wisdom brought two troubling observations. First, "everything done here under the sun is so irrational. Everything is meaningless, like chasing the wind" (Ecclesiastes 2:17). Sometimes work is monotonous. Sometimes life rewards diligence and hard work with failure. Sometimes work is a constant battle with unappreciative bosses, jealous coworkers, and petty bureaucrats. Work brings as much grief as it does joy.

Second, the one doing the work doesn't always enjoy the benefits. "I am disgusted that I must leave the fruits of my hard work to others. And who can tell whether my successors will be wise or foolish? And yet they will control everything I have gained by my skill and hard work. How meaningless!" (2:18-19). Perhaps Solomon had his own son Rehoboam in mind. This foolish son soon split apart the kingdom his father had worked so hard to build. No doubt Solomon had seen the seeds of irresponsibility growing in his son and could anticipate the unpleasant results.

Some individuals work hard throughout life, putting up with grief, misery, and other frustrations to gain the material benefits hard work can bring. But they wake up one day to realize their spouses and children are strangers. They have gained material possessions but forfeited the relationships that really mattered. Others work hard to provide for themselves and their children and work themselves into an early grave. Rather than being a means to an end, work becomes an end in itself and exacts a harsh toll from those who have allowed it to enslave them. Bottom line: Work did not bring the satisfaction and meaning Solomon had hoped for.

So What Brings Meaning to Life?

Does the book of Ecclesiastes contain nothing more than the angry words of a bitter man who realized too late he had squandered away his life? The answer is a resounding no! The portrait is not flattering, but Solomon must be brutally honest or the alluring glitz and glitter of life itself will crowd out the truth of his words. As hard as they are to hear, Solomon's observations on life have the ring of reality. These are still words of wisdom from a man who can speak from experience.

Solomon summarizes his wisdom for life in two basic statements. Instead of trying to "unscrew the inscrutable," (1) enjoy the life God has given you, and (2) trust and obey the God who does understand the meaning of life.

ENJOY LIFE

One key to living wisely in an uncertain world is to learn how to be satisfied with what God does supply. As a wise instructor, Solomon reemphasizes this theme throughout his book.

> I decided there is nothing better than to enjoy food and drink and to find satisfaction in work. Then I realized that this pleasure is from the hand of God. For who can

eat or enjoy anything apart from him? (Ecclesiastes 2:24-25)

I concluded that there is nothing better for people than to be happy and to enjoy themselves as long as they can. And people should eat and drink and enjoy the fruits of their labor, for these are gifts from God. (3:12-13)

I saw that there is nothing better for people than to be happy in their work. That is why they are here! No one will bring them back from death to enjoy life in the future. (3:22)

Even so, I have noticed one thing, at least, that is good. It is good for people to eat well, drink a good glass of wine, and enjoy their work—whatever they do under the sun—for however long God lets them live. And it is a good thing to receive wealth from God and the good health to enjoy it. To enjoy your work and accept your lot in life—that is indeed a gift from God. (5:18-19)

So I recommend having fun, because there is nothing better for people to do in this world than to eat, drink, and enjoy life. That way they will experience some happiness along with all the hard work God gives them. (8:15)

So go ahead. Eat your food and drink your wine with a happy heart, for God approves of this! Wear fine clothes, with a dash of cologne! Live happily with the woman you love through all the meaningless days of life that God has given you in this world. The wife God gives you is your reward for all your earthly toil. (9:7-9)

Observe closely Solomon's advice. Life from a human perspective is uncertain. You don't know how long you will live. You don't know if your hard work will bring material success. God has a plan for your life, but he does not reveal the details to you. So how does one live wisely in the midst of life's uncertainties? Solomon says one secret to a wise life is to recognize these uncertainties and then to enjoy the blessings God does bestow, rather than become angry or fearful of those things over which we have no control.

FEAR GOD

Some have described Solomon's first piece of advice as materialistic hedonism: Eat, drink, and be merry for tomorrow we may die! His words could be taken that way—were it not for the other piece of advice Solomon adds at the very end of his journal. We must understand his advice to enjoy life in the complete context of the book. First, he has already shown that a life dedicated only to the pursuit of pleasure will result in misery (Ecclesiastes 2). Second, he ends the book by pointing his readers beyond the materialism of this life to the reality of God and the life to come. These two restrictions form a set of mental bookends that limit the meaning one can give to his other words of advice.

Solomon reached the conclusion of his book by pointing his audience to the ultimate Source of the wisdom found within its pages. "The words of the wise are like goads, their collected sayings like firmly embedded nails—given by one Shepherd" (12:11, NIV). Each phrase emphasizes a unique aspect of the words contained in this book.

"Like goads" shows the *significance* of these words. Like a pointed stick used to prod a reluctant animal, Solomon chose his words to be as uncomfortable as they must sometimes be to push the reader forward on his or her spiritual journey.

"Like firmly embedded nails" shows the *stability* of these words. Like nails firmly fastened into wooden beams, Solomon's words will enable the reader to be anchored solidly in place rather than to be torn loose and blown about by life's uncertainties.

"Given by one Shepherd" shows the *source* of these words. Solomon may have spoken these words, but God is the ultimate Author. We can trust Solomon's words because they come from God.

What is God's final word on how to live wisely in uncertain times? "Here is my final conclusion: Fear God and obey his commands, for this is the duty of every person. God will judge us for everything we do, including every secret thing, whether good or bad" (12:13-14). The wise remember that God is in charge and that he will work everything out in his own way. We are not responsible to understand why everything in life happens as it does. But we are responsible to trust him in spite of life's circumstances.

Solomon's secret to wisdom? Wisdom begins when we develop a proper relationship to God—recognizing our limitations and humbly following his divine directives.

"Fear of the Lord is the beginning of knowledge. Only fools despise wisdom and discipline" (Proverbs 1:7).

Questions to Ponder

We tend to associate wisdom with knowledge. But a wise individual is one who understands from God's perspective how life works. Take some time to focus on several pointed questions related to practical wisdom.

1. Are you a workaholic? Does work take priority over your family or your time with the Lord?
2. If so, what can you do this week to bring more balance to your life?
3. What temptations are you facing in your life right now? What is the wisest way biblically to handle those problems?
4. Memorize Proverbs 1:7, and ask God to develop his wisdom in your life as you seek to trust and obey him.

This "foolish" plan of God is far wiser than the wisest of human plans, and God's weakness is far stronger than the greatest of human strength. (1 Corinthians 1:25)

4

SELF-CONTROL

If My Spirit Is Willing,
Why Is My Flesh So Weak?

Who's in Control?

Discipline is a dirty word! At least that's the impression we give by our inability to exercise self-control. I'm sitting at my "desk"—a small folding table set up in our living room—desperately looking for an opening illustration, but it's hard to concentrate with the "discussion" taking place between my wife and my daughter. Though my daughter has been up for over two hours, she has not yet made her bed. As my daughter leans over the balcony to argue her point, she pulls out the strongest argument she can muster. "Why should I make up my bed when twelve hours later I'll just mess it up again?" Creative—but ineffective against her mother!

Every parent who desires to fashion his or her child into a responsible adult is painfully aware of the struggle over self-control. Parenting is the process of moving children from external discipline to internal discipline—and at times they seem to move at the approximate speed of a glacier!

But why worry about self-control? Our society champions an individual's right to freedom and self-expression. "If it feels good, do it!" "Let it all hang out!" Doesn't too much emphasis on self-control stifle creativity, inhibit freedom, and squeeze the fun out of life? Not necessarily.

True self-control doesn't hinder freedom; it promotes freedom! Alcoholics have no self-control in their consumption of alcohol—and it enslaves them. By his own admission, Magic Johnson, the Los Angeles Lakers basketball star, exercised little or no self-control in his sex life. His incredible basketball career was cut short when he reported to the world he was HIV positive. His attempts to return to the court are only shadows of what might have been—had he exercised more self-control.

Absolute freedom, without any self-control, will *always* produce chaos. We must balance rights with responsibilities, or individual freedom will result in personal tragedy. The personal tragedy of Thomas "Hollywood" Henderson, who played football for the Dallas Cowboys, illustrates the sad reality of freedom without self-control. Henderson was a gifted athlete who never achieved his potential because of his involvement in drugs.

> As he would later admit, Thomas Henderson was not, due to drugs, in control. Henderson walked a fine line and had been warned by Landry to straighten up, but he seemed to have lost complete reality somewhere over the rainbow. . . .
>
> Henderson finally admitted his problems with drugs and then served time in a federal prison for a charge in which

two women, one in a wheelchair, accused him of assaulting them.[1]

Self-control provides the boundaries within which true freedom and creativity can flourish. It brings a maturity that allows an individual to say no to some things so that he or she can say yes to those things that are more significant, helpful, or necessary. When Stephen Covey wrote the runaway best-seller, *The 7 Habits of Highly Effective People,* he stressed the importance of commitment and self-control.

> As we make and keep commitments, even small commitments, we begin to establish an inner integrity that gives us the awareness of self-control and the courage and strength to accept more of the responsibility for our own lives. By making and keeping promises to ourselves and others . . . our honor becomes greater than our moods.[2]

Eat Your Vegetables!

Every parent knows the "airplane method" of feeding little children. The child, like a condemned prisoner, is strapped into the high chair. On the table, just out of reach, are the jars of strained, pureed, and otherwise mutilated vegetables that no self-respecting adult would ever eat! We pour the contents into the proper bins in the feeding plate and secure the plate to the high-chair tray with suction cups to prevent "accidental spills." And how do we get reluctant children to eat the necessary amount of pureed spinach and squash? We trick them. "Here comes the plane into the hangar! Open wide!"

The child grows, the style of chair changes, and the plate and utensils become more "adult" in appearance. But the hassle over vegetables continues. "No dessert until you eat those peas and carrots!" The struggle still remains to get children to do what they *need* to do rather than what they *want* to do. Given a reasonable choice, few children would ever choose peas and carrots over cookies and ice cream without some form of encouragement. The war to establish self-discipline is a series of such battles.

Newsweek magazine featured the subject of "Virtue" on June 13, 1994. The article highlighted the growing concern over the moral decline in Western society. Nothing epitomized more the sad state of moral decline than *Newsweek*'s need to include a separate article by its religion editor defining *virtue*. It's a word that has gone out of circulation in our society. Kenneth L. Woodward highlighted four cardinal virtues, one of which was temperance. Again, *temperance* needed to be defined. "And temperance involves much more than moderation in drink. It is self-discipline, the control of all the human passions and sensual pleasures—anger and frustration as well as food, drink, and sex."[3]

I'm out of Control!

Self-discipline sounds great in theory, but try putting it into practice! Try telling a hormone-driven eighteen-year-old boy to control his thought life. Or try telling the frazzled mother of energetic two-year-old twins to control her frustration. Life's pressures and difficulties sometimes catch us in their viselike grip and squeeze until we feel as though we will explode. Every nerve ending seems rubbed raw; every ounce of strength is sapped by these problems that hang on us like weights and suck out our strength like leeches. How can we develop self-control in a world that seems to do everything possible to titillate, tempt, test, and try our patience at every turn?

One wrong response to the struggle over self-control is to set up legalistic barriers—using external controls to regulate an internal problem. After Ayatollah Khomeini and his Islamic-fundamentalist allies took control in Iran, they imposed strict Moslem law and external controls over behavior. Women were no longer allowed to dress in "provocative" Western styles. Instead, the authorities required women to wear the *chador,* a dark robe that covers the entire body. Possession of pornography became a crime punishable by death.

Did such draconian measures solve the problem of sexual self-control? No! The regime still struggles vainly to plug the many loopholes in the law and impose their external moral standards. One of the most recent decisions was to ban satellite dishes. It seems thousands of homes were receiving X-rated movies and other sexually explicit programs through these dishes. External controls do not provide a long-term solution to the problem.

Tiny Tim

The essential struggles we face have not changed through the years because human nature has not changed. Two millennia ago the apostle Paul wrote to a young man in western Turkey struggling with some of the same problems facing us today. Timothy was the young protégé of the apostle Paul. He traveled with Paul on his journeys and learned much from this great apostle.

Life with Paul must have been both exciting and stressful for young Timothy. Paul's own description of his ministry leaves no doubt that it was not for the faint of heart.

> I have worked harder, been put in jail more often, been whipped times without number, and faced death again and again. Five different times the Jews gave me thirty-nine lashes. Three times I was beaten with rods. Once I was stoned. Three times I was shipwrecked. Once I spent a whole night and a day adrift at sea. I have traveled many weary miles. I have faced danger from flooded rivers and from robbers. I have faced danger from my own people, the Jews, as well as from the Gentiles. I have faced danger in the cities, in the deserts, and on the stormy seas. And I have faced danger from men who claim to be Christians but are not. (2 Corinthians 11:23-26)

Traveling with Paul was like serving on the front lines in a war. Always on the go. Always in harm's way. One hair-raising adventure after another. Paul had a mission from God, and Timothy did his best to keep up with his dynamic mentor. But being around Paul was intimidating. And Timothy was painfully aware of each perceived shortcoming.

Timothy must have felt like the Rodney Dangerfield of church leadership. In a society that valued age and equated it with wisdom, Timothy was a mere lad (1 Timothy 4:12). In a culturally segregated society, Timothy was the product of a religiously and racially mixed marriage—a believing Jewish mother and a pagan Gentile father (Acts 16:1). In a church that needed vigorous, powerful leaders, Timothy was timid and subject to frequent illness (1 Timothy 5:23; 2 Timothy 1:6-8).

Imagine Timothy's concern when the apostle Paul left him alone in Ephesus as his official representative. Paul expected Timothy to handle some serious problems that threatened to fragment this strategic church. To add to the stress, times were tough for all the churches in the Roman Empire. The number of believers in Jesus Christ had grown to the point that the authorities in Rome were now taking notice. Sometime after leaving Timothy in Ephesus, the apostle Paul was arrested, taken to Rome, and imprisoned by the Roman government for a second time. This imprisonment probably ended with his execution.

Timothy inherited a church that was floundering because of false teaching and defections from the faith. Some advocated rigid, external obedience to restrictive laws as the way to achieve self-control and acceptance with God. "They will say it is wrong to be married and wrong to eat certain foods" (1 Timothy 4:3). Others promoted self-centered philosophies based on vain speculation. Paul expected young, struggling Timothy to model the message of biblical self-discipline to these people. Paul shared three specific secrets with Timothy for developing self-discipline in himself and others.

Secret #1: Fall in Love with Jesus Christ

A magical transformation takes place in a young man's life sometime during his teenage years. Those "yucky girls" whose pigtails he once pulled suddenly become interesting, exciting—desirable! It's as if the poles of a magnet are reversed. The long-haired cootie-carriers that used to repel now seem irresistibly attractive. That's *amoré!*

Wise King Solomon also observed this change in young men's lives. He compared a man's changing behavior when he notices a woman to the mysterious, untraceable movements of an eagle, a snake, and a sailing ship. "There are three things that amaze me—no, four things I do not understand: how an eagle glides through the sky, how a snake slithers on a rock, how a ship navigates the ocean, how a man loves a woman" (Proverbs 30:18-19).

How a man loves a woman! Love certainly does cause changes in actions and attitudes. A young man in love starts caring about his overall personal appearance—his clothing, his hair, his complexion. His use of deodorant and cologne increases dramatically. Moms stand in awe, mouths hanging open, as their sons *willingly* assume responsibility for their personal appearance.

The desire to please someone we love is a powerful motivational force. The patriarch Jacob worked for seven long years to gain permission to marry Rachel, "but his love for her was so strong that it seemed to him but a few days" (Genesis 29:20). If you love someone deeply, you willingly limit your freedom because your greater desire is to please that person. Self-control flows easily from a heart of love.

The apostle Paul understood this secret for developing self-control. In leaving Timothy in Ephesus, Paul urged him to stop the spread of false teaching. Timothy was to promote God's true message in the church. "The purpose of my instruction is that all the Christians there would be filled with love that comes from a pure heart, a clear conscience, and sincere faith" (1 Timothy 1:5).

Paul knew firsthand the power of love. As a zealous Pharisee on the road to Damascus, he experienced God's love—and it changed his life. Paul unflinchingly described himself before he knew Jesus Christ: "I used to scoff at the name of Christ. I hunted down his people, harming them in every way I could" (1:13). God extended his grace to someone deserving only judgment, and Paul's debt of love motivated him to serve his Lord.

How much do you love the Lord? Another apostle, John, reminded his readers of the order in which love develops. "We love . . . as a result of his loving us first" (1 John 4:19). The more you realize the depth of God's love for you—a love so deep he willingly sent his Son to die for your sins—the more you will grow in your love for him. And the more you love him, the more willing you will be to make those changes in your life that will please him.

Secret #2: Live Out the Word of God

Racquetball is a fast-paced sport that could be described as kamikaze tennis. Up to four people stand in a small room, swinging short racquets at a hollow rubber ball. The ball bounces wildly off the floor, ceiling, and four walls. Each player tries to hit the ball off the front wall in a way that denies the other player(s) an opportunity to make a return shot.

I love the game. (My wife insists that says something about my personal sanity.) I wear the welts left by the ball's hitting my back and arms as badges of honor from hard-fought matches. I'm the oldest player in our regular four-some—but I can hold my own in a game!

The secret in racquetball is knowing where the ball will bounce after hitting the front wall—and anticipating your opponent's next shot. A strong, quick, but inexperienced racquetball player will usually lose to a more knowledge-able opponent, even if that opponent is older, slower, and weaker. Knowledge and skill are more important than strength and speed. Mastering the disciplines of the game gives a player an edge.

Paul wrote to Timothy to give him the knowledge and skill he needed to direct the church at Ephesus. Timothy needed to master the skills essential for becoming an effective leader. In 1 Timothy 4:6, Paul shared with Timothy the vital link between self-discipline and the Word of God: Paul began by reminding Timothy that he had been "fed by the message of faith and the true teaching." Before Timothy could serve as a "worthy servant of Christ Jesus," he had to know the truth of God's Word. Mastering the fundamentals is essential for developing self-discipline.

But knowing and teaching the truth of God's Word is

not enough. The truth must move from our head to our heart to our hands. Timothy was not only to "teach these things and insist that everyone learn them," Paul also expected him to "be an example to all believers" (4:11-12).

Paul listed five specific areas in which Timothy needed to develop self-discipline. Each is important.

- *Speech:* Be an example in what you say.
- *Life:* Be an example in what you do.
- *Love:* Be an example in how you help others.
- *Faith:* Be an example in how you trust God.
- *Purity:* Be an example in how you relate to the opposite sex.

I suspect young Timothy's eyes widened as he read through this list. His throat tightened, and his heart started racing in his chest. Paul wanted self-discipline in *every* area of life. How could Timothy possibly remember all these requirements?

Paul's answer follows. "Until I get there, focus on reading the Scriptures to the church, encouraging the believers, and teaching them" (4:13). As Timothy immersed himself in God's Word, he would find the answers he needed to develop self-discipline, both in himself and in the lives of God's people in Ephesus.

God's Word provides the knowledge we need to live in a way that pleases God. The more we study God's Word and make it part of our thought process, the more we will be able to live lives characterized by self-discipline.

When my two children were much younger, I once took them to "play" racquetball. They swung wildly at the ball and ran to the right as the ball bounced off the wall toward the left. They had fun—but they didn't play racquetball! They lacked the basic knowledge of how to play the game. And without that knowledge they could not be successful. Our Christian lives are the same. We need a knowledge of God's Word if we hope to live successfully. It's hard to exercise self-discipline if we don't know which areas of our life we need to develop. Only God's Word gives us that truth.

Secret #3: Don't Fall into Legalism

Our "hurry-up" society has mastered the thirty-second sound bite. As life becomes more complex, we long for simplistic answers. Many vote for their state and national leaders based on television commercials that are long on style and short on substance. We expect television networks to summarize national and international news to the point that we can learn what's happening in the world in half an hour.

We take a similar approach to biblical self-discipline. Self-discipline takes so long to develop the old-fashioned way. Can't we reduce God's expectations for our lives to the "top ten" or "big five" commands he wants us to follow? It would be so much easier to live a life of self-discipline if all we had to remember was, "Don't drink, smoke, and chew—or go with girls who do!"

A ready-made list of dos and don'ts for living the Christian life sounds inviting, but the results are devastating.

Eventually the list of dos and don'ts becomes more important than God's Word. The Pharisees started out with a noble desire. They wanted to build a hedge around God's Word lest they accidentally violate a command and sin against God. Their specific lists of dos and don'ts were fences designed to help them and their followers stay inside God's law.

Unfortunately, by the time of Jesus this list of dos and don'ts had grown to the point where it harmed those who tried to keep the rules. Jesus reserved some of his harshest condemnations for those who preached such legalism. "They crush you with impossible religious demands and never lift a finger to help ease the burden" (Matthew 23:4). In the same passage, Jesus called the Pharisees hypocrites, blind guides, blind fools, whitewashed tombs, snakes, and sons of vipers!

Why such harsh words? Jesus condemned those who promote legalism because legalism inevitably does just the opposite of what it sets out to do. Instead of helping define the Word of God, it replaces the Word of God with human rules. Instead of providing freedom to do what is right, it enslaves in a system too burdensome to bear. Instead of promoting righteousness, it fosters hypocritical pride. Instead of leading to life, it ultimately results in death.

Don't get me wrong. The opposite of legalism is *not* lawlessness—it's the standards of righteousness found in God's Word. Legalism takes the Word of God and adds to it. It substitutes specific human rules for those ordained by God.

I see two very specific differences between legalism and

the standards set by God. First, legalism tries to set tighter boundaries than God imposes. For example, God had told Israel to "remember to observe the Sabbath day by keeping it holy" (Exodus 20:8). The legalism of the Pharisees told Israel how they could eat on the Sabbath (Matthew 12:1-2), what they could—and could not—carry on the Sabbath (John 5:10), and how far they could walk on the Sabbath (Acts 1:12). They added shackles to the law of God.

Second, legalism leads to the belief that keeping a specific list of laws will make a person righteous. But God's Word says we should try to live a righteous life because God has *already* made us righteous. Legalism holds out the promise of earning favor with God by following a set of rules. Biblical self-discipline encourages us to obey God's Word so our life can match our settled position as God's children.

Legalism is not something new. The Pharisees practiced it in Christ's day, and some individuals tried to impose it on the church in Ephesus. Paul warned Timothy of the danger of substituting legalism for self-discipline. The false teachers in Ephesus stressed obedience to the law (1 Timothy 1:7-11). Paul reminded Timothy that "[the laws] were not made for people who do what is right. They are for people who are disobedient and rebellious, who are ungodly and sinful, who consider nothing sacred and defile what is holy, who murder their father or mother or other people" (1:9).

Law can help hold evil in check, but it can't produce righteousness. Law puts criminals in prison—but it doesn't make those who are already righteous more godly.

Paul reminded Timothy of the motives behind many

individuals who promote legalism. "These teachers are hypocrites and liars. They pretend to be religious, but their consciences are dead" (4:2). Harsh words. True words. People who add their standards of right and wrong to the Word of God are usurping the place of God.

Paul gave two specific examples of the legalism creeping into the church at Ephesus. "They will say it is wrong to be married and wrong to eat certain foods" (4:3). Perhaps these teachers thought that forbidding all marriage would solve the problem of sexual immorality. It didn't! Perhaps they thought a list of forbidden foods would keep them from offending others. It wouldn't! The only thing these additional lists of rules accomplished was to take the very things God created as good and call them evil. Legalism was *not* the route Timothy needed to take to develop self-discipline.

Get on God's Exercise Program

Though Timothy had faithfully served with Paul for nearly a decade, he still needed to continue developing self-discipline in his life. Paul reminded him of the need to "spend your time and energy in training yourself for spiritual fitness" (1 Timothy 4:7). The process takes time—and effort. Paul shared three specific secrets for developing self-control. The first two were positive. Falling in love with Jesus Christ motivates the believer to make those changes that will please his or her Lord. Spending time in God's Word will reveal those areas of our lives that need to change—and will give us the knowledge we need to be conformed to the image of our God.

Paul also provided a third secret: Avoid the shortcut of legalism. Self-control is more than slavishly following a list of rules. Such an approach seems both logical and helpful—but it ultimately enslaves those who fall under its spell.

Questions to Ponder

Self-control is a by-product of God's ministry in our lives. "When the Holy Spirit controls our lives, he will produce this kind of fruit in us: . . . self-control" (Galatians 5:22-23). We can aid in the process as we come to know and love God and his Word.

1. How much do you love the Lord? Read Philippians 2, and pause to think about all Jesus did for you. Then stop to thank the Lord and express your love to God.
2. Are you spending time in God's Word? If not, consider committing to reading at least one chapter of the Bible every day. You could start with Paul's letters to Timothy.
3. Do you know individuals who have a set of rules they expect all others to follow? Be very careful about falling into the trap of legalism.
4. Memorize Galatians 5:22-23, and compare your life to the fruit of the Spirit described there.

Spend your time and energy in training yourself for spiritual fitness. Physical exercise has some value, but spiritual exercise is much more important, for it promises a reward in both this life and the next. (1 Timothy 4:7-8)

5

JOY

Is Laughter the Best Medicine?

Grumpy Old Men

Everyone liked to visit Aunt Hannah, but most dreaded talking with Uncle Paul. This childless couple was the last of my father's aunts and uncles who lived nearby. Aunt Hannah reminded me of Aunt Bea on the original *Andy Griffith Show*. She was a warmhearted, matronly woman who prepared some of the best home-cooked meals I ever tasted—from the perfectly cooked roast to the lumpless gravy to the flaky crust on her homemade apple pie. Going to Aunt Hannah's for dinner was fun—except for Uncle Paul.

Uncle Paul could have auditioned for a part in the movie *Grumpy Old Men*. If his life had been a fiddle, it would have played only two songs: "Call Me Irresponsible," and "Stormy Weather." He spent much of his life squandering his time and money on silly pursuits and hobbies, only to abandon them after a short time. He had photographs in albums he never viewed, 8-mm movies he never watched, and model airplanes he had long ago stopped flying. By the end of his life his major activities were describing how wonderful he had been in the past and how many physical ailments and problems he now had.

Dad always issued a standard warning before we went to visit Aunt Hannah and Uncle Paul. "Don't ask Uncle Paul how he feels!" That was a recipe for disaster. I know because one time I forgot and asked. His detailed description of the surgical removal of most of his stomach did wonders to my appetite—especially since the description lasted for most of the meal! When we left later that evening, he was still describing the various operations, ailments, and medications around which his life revolved. I never again asked him how he felt!

After I left home and moved away to college, I still visited Aunt Hannah and Uncle Paul when I came home. Every visit ended the same way. As I was saying good-bye, Uncle Paul would come over and say, "Yeah, I'd better say good-bye. I just might not be here when you get back this way again to visit." And he was not talking about moving to Maui! This continued for fifteen years.

Uncle Paul finally died, and I went back home for the funeral. Two sad thoughts played on my mind while I was there. First, I could not recall being with Uncle Paul one single time when he was actually joyful or having a good time. Instead, I remembered him for his self-centeredness and self-pity. Second, I wondered how many of those in attendance would have come to Uncle Paul's funeral had it not been for Aunt Hannah. More came to pay their respects to her than to honor him.

All of us have our own Uncle Pauls. One comic strip even revolves around the life of a classic, crotchety old man. It's called "Crankshaft," and it can be brutally funny. Imagine reading the following comic on a cold February morning.

Panel One: A dark house is silhouetted next to a barren tree. A fierce snowstorm howls all around, while light pours from one window in the house. From inside the house comes the following comment: "It sure feels good to be inside on a night like this . . ."

Panel Two: The reader is taken inside the house. The husband and wife are seated on their sofa. The husband curls his arm around his wife's neck while she continues her sentence from the previous panel, ". . . with the winter wind howling outside . . ."

Panel Three: A voice shouts from another room, "Who got rid of the newspapers!? How can I start a fire without newspapers!?" The husband turns to his wife and finishes her sentence for her: ". . . and your dad howling inside!"

The world is full of Ed Crankshafts, whose mission in life is to suck joy from all they meet. And many do so in the name of Christ! They somehow equate a sour disposition and a furrowed brow with spiritual maturity. How sad.

It's Just a Joke!

When Chuck Swindoll came to Dallas Theological Seminary as president, the first thing he unpacked was his sense of humor. The president's office is on the first floor of Davidson Hall. Before Chuck arrived, a student, knowing Chuck's love for Harley-Davidson motorcycles, put a sign over the front entrance next to the building name. For that short time, Davidson Hall became Harley-Davidson Hall. A few of the more serious types took offense at this breach in propriety, but Chuck just howled with laughter.

One thing I love about Chuck is his willingness to shake up a crowd with some outlandish statement—just to get a reaction from a group that's being too serious. Then as their heads snap up and their jaws drop to the floor, he'll say, "It's just a joke!" He shared with me some wise advice that I have been trying to incorporate into my own life. "I take the Word of God very seriously, but I'm learning not to take myself so seriously."

I remember as a child receiving a new wind-up watch. I made sure I wound the watch every morning. I was always concerned that the watch might wind down overnight, so I wound the spring as tight as I could every day. Unfortunately I kept the tension on the spring so tight that eventually the spring snapped, and the watch quit running. People, like watches, can also get wound too tight. And when they do, they snap.

Watches—and people—are designed to work, to keep moving, to have hands that are in motion. The secret to longevity is not inactivity but balance. Tension and stress must be balanced with some flexibility that enables one to spring back.

Lives that are stressed out, frazzled, and wound too tight

need a break that will provide some sense of balance. One remedy prescribed by God is joy.

Living *above* the Circumstances

"So, Frank, how's it going?" "OK, under the circumstances." Ever have that conversation? Most of us have. We see our lives and well-being tied to circumstances that swirl out of control around us. Advertisers assault us with the message that true happiness comes from purchasing a new car, buying a new wardrobe, or finding a new romantic interest. The subtle message is that to be happy we need to change our circumstances.

If circumstances dictate happiness, how happy would you be serving a four-year prison sentence for a crime you didn't commit? Imagine how you would feel if, during that time, you watched your already shaky financial situation slip further into the red. Then imagine how you would respond to news that a very close friend who had faithfully come to visit you was ill and at the point of death. No freedom—no financial security—no way to help a friend in need. *Under the circumstances* you might well be discouraged and depressed, to say the least! But the one who faced these problems was not "under the circumstances"— he lived above them. He was the apostle Paul.

The Jewish religious leaders attacked Paul in Jerusalem during a visit to the temple (Acts 21). The Roman garrison that arrested him actually saved his life by rescuing him from a mob planning to stone him to death. The religious leaders lodged trumped-up charges against Paul, and he spent two years awaiting trial at the coastal city of Caesarea

(23:33-35; 24:27). After two years the religious leaders asked to have Paul brought back to Jerusalem, but they planned to ambush the garrison along the way and kill Paul. Exercising his privileges and rights as a Roman citizen, Paul appealed to Caesar to have his case decided in Rome. After a hair-raising voyage across the Mediterranean (including a shipwreck on Malta!), Paul arrived in Rome only to spend another two years under house arrest awaiting the arrival of his accusers. Paul lost four years of his life for a crime he never committed. *Under the circumstances* we could expect Paul to become bitter and disillusioned, but he didn't!

Rome had a unique plan to control prison overpopulation and lower the cost of maintaining their prison system. The Roman authorities allowed some prisoners to live in homes under "house arrest." The prisoner was responsible to pay for the housing and meals, but he was not allowed to leave the home to work. (In fact, he was chained to a Roman guard during this imprisonment!) Paul was given the privilege of being under house arrest (28:16, 30). The only problem was getting the money to pay for the house!

In the best of times, Paul received adequate finances for his ministry. He could work as a tentmaker, and some churches sent financial contributions to help him in his ministry. But at other times the work disappeared and the financial contributions dried up. Paul knew the best—and worst—of financial times. "I know how to live on almost nothing or with everything," he wrote. The breadth of situations faced by Paul included having "a full stomach or empty, with plenty or little" (Philippians 4:12). Unable to work while confined to house arrest, responsible for his own lodging and living expenses, not receiving any financial support from churches where he had labored so diligently—*under the circumstances* we could expect Paul to become discouraged. But he didn't!

A gift finally arrived from the church in Philippi. Hand-carried by a personal friend of Paul, the gift was as refreshing as a cold drink of water on a hot day. But that brief moment of happiness was shattered when Epaphroditus, this courier and friend, fell ill. All Paul's prayers and all Dr. Luke's medical skills seemed unable to stop the illness that wrapped its arms around Epaphroditus and pulled him ever closer to the abyss of death. *Under the circumstances* we could expect Paul to be disheartened and give up. But he didn't!

Pen in hand, Paul sat down to write to the congregation that had shared so generously with him. Chains clanking as he shuffled around the room, Paul dictated one of the most upbeat letters found in the New Testament—the Epistle to the Philippians. *Under the circumstances* we wouldn't expect Paul to focus on the theme of joy. But he did!

Rejoice in the Lord Always!

How could Paul ever find such joy in the problems he faced? The church in Philippi must have wondered how Paul could survive emotionally the many persecutions, trials, and injustices he had undergone. Imagine their surprise when they received his heartening letter!

Paul's secret to joy was to look beyond his circumstances to the Lord. Problems come and go. Circumstances constantly change. But God is unchangeable, and his plan is unalterable. Looking to God can provide stability and hope—and this leads to joy.

Paul began his letter by sharing the secret for his great confidence and joy. "Every time I think of you, I give thanks to my God. . . . I am sure that God, who began the good work within you, will continue his work until it is finally finished on that day when Christ Jesus comes back again" (Philippians 1:3, 6). Paul wasn't wringing his hands in emotional agony over what would happen to these churches in his absence. God was in charge, and Paul could depend on God to work everything out.

And yet, sometimes it's easier to trust God for what he will do in *others'* lives than it is to trust him to work in *our* life. How can we be joyful when we are being personally attacked, maligned, and misunderstood? We can almost hear Paul's friends in Philippi whisper this question to themselves. After all, there were some scoundrels in Rome preaching in the name of Christ just to cause problems for Paul. And Paul could do nothing to stop them. Would he be discouraged, angry, perhaps even bitter over this gross injustice? Not Paul!

"But whether or not their motives are pure, the fact remains that the message about Christ is being preached, so I rejoice. . . . For to me, living is for Christ, and dying is even better" (1:18, 21). Instead of being discouraged, Paul was *excited* about those who were preaching Christ in order to cause trouble for him.

Look at the big picture! he told his readers. More people are sharing Christ than ever before!

But what if they cause so much trouble you are put to death?

If I die, I win! I'll be with Christ in heaven forever!

Paul was joyful because he viewed his circumstances from God's perspective. He wasn't *under the circumstances;* he was looking above them to see what God was doing.

Paul seems to have stressed two themes relating to the joy he had in the Lord. The first is the fact that he could rejoice because he knew the Lord was in charge. He saw the hand of God in everything taking place—even those events that caused him temporary discomfort or difficulty. Thus he could take his concerns to the Lord and trust the Lord to work them out. Paul's second theme is the fact that he knew the Lord could return at any time. His problems were just temporary inconveniences that would soon be replaced by permanent fellowship with the Lord.

Both themes join together in Paul's exhortation to live lives of joyful expectation and trust.

Always be full of joy in the Lord. I say it again—rejoice! Let everyone see that you are considerate in all you do. Remember, the Lord is coming soon.

Don't worry about anything; instead, pray about everything. Tell God what you need, and thank him for all he has done. If you do this, you will experience God's peace, which is far more wonderful than the human mind can understand. His peace will guard your hearts and minds as you live in Christ Jesus. (4:4-7)

Recently I flew back to Pennsylvania to speak in a church near where I grew up. I stayed in my parents' home for the weekend. Mom was away for the first two days of my visit, so Dad and I spent some quality time together. It was probably the first extended time we had shared alone together in over twenty years.

Dad and I drove to the farm where he spent his childhood. The air was cool and crisp, some trees were red with the first blush of fall, and the stalks of corn rustled their brown leaves in the noonday sun. We finally stopped the car at the end of a dirt road on the bank of Big Roaring Creek. The buildings were gone, but their locations were firmly etched in Dad's mind. The farmhouse, the barn, the icehouse, the pigpen, and the sawmill all came to life under his contemplative gaze. Then we walked down to the dam, and my memories joined with those of my dad.

Generations often have little in common, but Dad and I share childhood memories of Big Roaring Creek—the "swimmin' hole" he and I both remember from our youth. Dad taught me to swim there, just as he had learned to swim there as a child. Memories flow deep in that stream.

I remember the bone-chilling, goose-bump-raising temperature of the water when I would jump in for the first time during a family picnic. The current seemed strong, the water seemed deep, and the rocks seemed sharp and jagged as I stood on the edge of the falls preparing to dive. But whenever I became momentarily paralyzed by fear, I would just look out into the water and see Dad watching me. He was ready to come to my rescue, if needed. Knowing he was near—and watching—took away any anxiety and gave me the freedom to press on.

Paul experienced the same sense of freedom. The Lord was near—and watching. Paul could face life with confidence and joy because he understood the power and presence of God.

Rejoice in Serving Others

When I was a young child, a Sunday school teacher taught me the secret to spelling *JOY* in the Christian life: *J*esus first, *O*thers second, *Y*ourself last. Paul may not have known the jingle, but he understood the idea. Much of his joy came from putting the Lord first in his life and viewing life from God's perspective. But Paul also understood the second principle that leads to joy—putting others ahead of ourselves.

Pausing to choose his words carefully, Paul boldly asked the Philippians to make his joy complete "by agreeing wholeheartedly with each other, loving one another, and working together with one heart and purpose." He gave further instructions on how to do this: "Don't be selfish; don't live to make a good impression on others. Be humble, thinking of others as better than yourself" (Philippians 2:2-3).

Some of the saddest individuals alive today are people who think only of themselves. They are so self-absorbed that they have no understanding of the personal satisfaction they can receive in serving others.

Paul realized that the best way to teach the people of Philippi this truth was to wrap it in human form. We learn best when we can observe specific examples. As the old saying goes, "Some things are better caught than taught." Paul provided four specific examples of individuals who found joy in serving others.

EXAMPLE #1: JESUS

The apostle used Jesus as his first example. "Your attitude should be the same that Christ Jesus had" (Philippians 2:5). Jesus was willing to give up his rightful place in heaven to lay aside his glory and become a man. As the God-man he took on the role of servant and willingly gave his life on the cross to purchase eternal life for others. In arguing from the greater to the lesser Paul emphasized that if the Son of God was willing to give up his rightful place in heaven to serve us, we ought to be willing to give up some of our "rights" to serve others.

EXAMPLE #2: PAUL

Most—perhaps all—of Paul's readers had never met Jesus during his time on earth. They knew what Jesus had done, but some may have had trouble relating to his example because Jesus was the perfect God-man while they struggled as "mere mortals." As if anticipating their objection, Paul moved quickly to his second example—himself!

Paul introduced this second example by urging his readers, "In everything you do, stay away from complaining and arguing" (Philippians 2:14). They were to be different from the rest of society. Living in the midst of the "crooked and perverse people" of their day, individuals who could display joyful contentment would "shine brightly" (2:15). Paul then used his own response to his four-year imprisonment as an example for them to follow. His willingness to share God's Good News with individuals like those in Philippi had put him in prison, on trial for his very life. "But even if my life is to be poured out like a drink offering to complete the sacrifice of your faithful service (that is, if I am to die for you), I will rejoice, and I want to share my joy with all of you" (2:17). His service for others brought joy.

Never underestimate the power of a personal example. As I mentioned earlier, about five years ago I decided to take up golf. It was a wise man who observed that *golf* is merely *flog* spelled backward! I still measure my progress by the number of balls lost per round. ("Well, I'm eight under for the day!") I know I could not have made it through those first humiliating months had it not been for Greg Hatteberg.

Greg works at Dallas Theological Seminary, and his middle name should be Barnabas—"son of encouragement." He patiently took me golfing and encouraged me through each round. Watching him, I not only learned the fundamentals of golf, I also learned how to relax, unwind, and *enjoy* the game—in spite of my mistakes. But Greg taught me more than golf. God used him as a living example of the joy one can experience in serving others.

EXAMPLE #3: TIMOTHY

Paul's third example was his protégé, Timothy. Timothy remembered Philippi well! After joining Paul early in his second missionary journey, (Acts 16:1-3), Timothy sailed with Paul from Asia Minor to Europe. Philippi was the first European city where Paul planted a church (16:12-40). Timothy experienced the early revival, the satanic opposition, the unruly mob, and the ugly beating and imprisonment. He also shook with the force of the earthquake that rocked the city and sprung open the door of the jail holding Paul and Silas. During a later missionary journey, Paul sent Timothy and another disciple back to Philippi as his special envoys (19:21-22). The Philippians knew Timothy!

Paul introduced this third example by expressing his desire to send Timothy to Philippi on a fact-finding mission. But then the masterful teacher explained why he was so eager to send Timothy. "I have no one else like Timothy, who genuinely cares about your welfare. All the others care only for themselves and not for what matters to Jesus Christ. But you know how Timothy has proved himself" (Philippians 2:20-22). In effect, Paul says to the Philippians, Want a third example of selfless service for others? Think back and remember how Timothy conducted himself when he was with you!

Paul stresses three specific concerns that consumed Timothy. Timothy genuinely cared about the welfare of the church at Philippi (2:20), Timothy also focused on what mattered to Jesus Christ (2:21), and as a dutiful son he willingly served with Paul (2:22). The one area Timothy did *not* make a priority was his own interests (2:21). Timothy had shown the Philippians how to spell *JOY: Jesus* first, *Others* second, *Yourself* last.

EXAMPLE #4: EPAPHRODITUS

Paul's gallery of godly examples is impressive. Jesus, Paul himself, and Timothy. But Paul saved the most obvious example for last. Paul's letter to the Philippians was hand carried by Epaphroditus—one of their own members. The church in Philippi had sent Epaphroditus on a mission of mercy to Paul in Rome. Along with kind words of greeting, this trusted messenger also carried a sizable offering from the church to help Paul with his living expenses during his time in prison.

Epaphroditus's kind actions almost turned to tragedy when he fell deathly ill during his stay in Rome. Paul pulled no punches in describing the gravity of the situation: "He surely was ill; in fact, he almost died" (Philippians 2:27). What caused this serious illness? Paul did not say specifically, but he implied that the illness resulted, in some measure, from his ministry to Paul. Epaphroditus "risked his life for the work of Christ, and he was at the point of death while trying to do for me the things you couldn't do because you were far away" (2:30).

I imagine Epaphroditus blushed when the letter was read aloud in the church and Paul singled him out by name. This unpretentious servant became more distressed over learning that his home church had heard he was ill than he did over the illness itself! Paul stressed the same three priorities in Epaphroditus that he had earlier used for Timothy: Epaphroditus focused on doing the work of Christ, on making a hazardous journey from Philippi to Rome to take care of Paul's needs, and on serving as the messenger from Philippi who could make up for the help the others could not give

Paul. Epaphroditus could also show the Philippians how to spell *JOY: J*esus first, *O*thers second, *Y*ourself last.

Humor Me

Joy in life begins with putting Jesus first. We learn to live *above* the circumstances as we come to know and love the God who controls all circumstances. Joy continues to grow as we focus on serving others rather than living to please ourselves. In extending a hand to help someone else, our sense of well-being grows. Just as exercise helps develop and build strong muscles, so service to others helps increase our joy.

The *J* is for Jesus, and the *O* is for others. But *JOY* is not complete without *Y*ou. Life is often serious, sometimes painful, frequently full of disappointments. The frustrations of life can suck energy—and joy—from even the most mature Christian.

While Jesus and others must be priorities, that doesn't mean you should neglect your own welfare. Replenish your reservoir of personal joy with frequent deposits of humor. Dr. Richard A. Swenson, a Christian physician, wrote an excellent book on the stress of modern life that threatens our emotional, physical, financial, and time reserves. One prescription he offers to counteract these pressures is laughter.

Humor is medicine. It tastes better than pills, it works as well, and it costs less. Why do you think children are so buoyant, so resilient, so capable of picking themselves up and going on? There are many reasons, and laughter is prominent among them.[1]

So how much have you laughed today? this week? Is your reservoir of inner laughter full and lapping over—or has the supply dwindled to critical levels? If so, call a friend who is always good for a laugh. Look through photo albums of joyful times in the past—and chuckle as you remember the laughter. Pull a book by Erma Bombeck off the shelf, and watch her discover laughter in everyday situations. Read the comics in your local paper—at least those that are still funny. But do *something* to exercise those muscles at the corners of your mouth!

Questions to Ponder

The old saying is still true: *JOY* is spelled *J*esus first, *O*thers second, and *Y*ourself last. Love Jesus, look for ways to serve others—and laugh!

1. Are there any specific problems or circumstances that seem to be sucking the joy from your life right now? If so, make a list of them. Can you trust Jesus to take care of all those problems? Pray over your list, and ask the Lord to help you see your problems from his perspective—to take you *above* your circumstances.
2. How are you serving others in your church or community? Plan one project you can do this week to help someone less fortunate than yourself.
3. When was the last time you laughed so hard you started to cry? What were you doing? Who was there? Call that person and tell him or her that you were just thinking about a great time you

once had together and wanted to call and share it again. Relive the experience with your friend—and laugh!

4. Memorize Philippians 4:4, and ask God to let your life reflect his joy.

A cheerful heart is good medicine, but a broken spirit saps a person's strength. (Proverbs 17:22)

6

T R U S T

Can I Depend on God?

From Beaver Cleaver to Bart Simpson

Western society has been rocked by a profound spiritual, social, and moral shift that began in the 1950s. Much of the shift in the United States can be attributed to the post–World War II baby-boom generation. In contrast to their parents, baby boomers came to adulthood

- fearing nuclear annihilation rather than the Great Depression or fascism
- opposing war in Vietnam rather than supporting World War II
- watching television rather than listening to radio
- equating the presidency with Watergate rather than the New Deal
- distrusting, rather than respecting, those in authority

I came of age in the turbulent 1960s, and I have watched the idealism (and radicalism!) of that time give way to a cynical, hard-bitten attitude today. The Beaver

Cleavers have become today's Bart Simpsons. And along the way we have lost our ability to trust.

In God We Trust

My struggles with trust took a dramatic turn the year I graduated from college. The year was 1974, a dramatic year, both in my life and in the life of the United States. The entire Watergate affair was lurching toward the climax that would force Richard Nixon from office on threat of impeachment. At the same time, an Arab oil embargo that raised the price and limited the supply of gasoline paralyzed much of America. I sat in a long line of cars in the early-morning darkness waiting—hoping—for the service station to open so I could fill my empty tank.

I was graduating from college in May, getting married in June, and moving across the country in August to begin studies at Dallas Theological Seminary. As spring approached I began questioning my decision to move to Dallas. How did I know this was what God wanted me to do? How could I be sure God would take care of me? Was this a wise move for Kathy and me? One of my problems was that I knew *no one* in Dallas. (I had never been farther south than Virginia, and neither had my wife.)

Everything we owned fit into a four-by-six-foot U-Haul—and most of that was books! As the time drew near for us to leave Washington, D. C., for Dallas, we scraped together all our resources. After paying off our college debts we had just enough money to drive to Dallas, rent a small apartment, buy a few weeks' worth of groceries, and pay for our first semester of seminary tuition. Hardly a nest egg!

How could we make such a move? Looking back at it today, it still seems rather remarkable. And yet I remember very specifically what gave me the peace, the faith, and the trust at that time. Earlier that spring I had started praying and asking God to be very specific in showing me what he wanted me to do. I had applied to Dallas Theological Seminary, and I told him that if he wanted me to go to Dallas, he would need to make it very clear.

During the time I was praying I was also reading through the book of Hebrews in my time alone with God. A few weeks after I asked God for a specific sense of direction, I came to Hebrews 11. One verse jumped off the page. "It was by faith that Abraham obeyed when God called him to leave home and go to another land that God would give him as his inheritance. He went without knowing where he was going" (Hebrews 11:8).

God used that verse in my life to teach me the meaning of faith and trust. Abraham was a man of faith who, when God directed him to do something, obeyed, even if he didn't fully understand all the details of what God was asking. He trusted God enough to know that God could take care of the details. That was the lesson I had to master during the spring and summer of 1974. Was my God big enough to take care of Kathy and me when we moved to Dallas? The answer, we discovered, was a resounding *yes!* God took us through that time and helped us grow very dramatically in our trust of him.

Not that it was always easy! For years I saved the check

register from that first year in Dallas. There were times when we had less than $5 in our checking account with more than a week left till payday. (We ate a *lot* of macaroni and cheese! It was cheap!) But in the midst of those difficult times God showed us repeatedly that he could— and would—meet our needs. We learned to trust because, as we stepped out in faith, we found that God was dependable.

By Faith Abraham . . .

Hebrews 11 is often called God's "Hall of Faith." The chapter mentions faith twenty-two times and illustrates it from the lives of at least sixteen specific individuals. The writer begins the chapter by defining the essence of faith. "What is faith? It is the confident assurance that what we hope for is going to happen. It is the evidence of things we cannot yet see" (11:1). Faith is the ability to trust in God and his promises before we see them come to pass.

In selecting Abraham, the writer chose an important example for his Jewish-Christian readers. Abraham was the physical and spiritual father of all Jews, and he lived a life characterized by faith. The author of Hebrews used Abraham to teach three specific lessons on faith.

FAITH FOLLOWS WHEN GOD CALLS

Our first glimpse of Abraham gives no hint of his later greatness. Had Ur of the Chaldees had a high school, the senior class would not have nominated Abraham as "Most Likely to Succeed." Abram (Abraham's original name) was one of three sons born into a pagan family. His father "worshiped other gods" (Joshua 24:2). Ur, the city of his birth, was a center for the worship of the moon god. Abram's brother Haran died, and Abram assumed responsibility for his surviving son. Abram married Sarai (Sarah's original name), but their inability to have children marred the marriage. Nothing in his background set Abraham apart as a remarkable man of faith.

What transformed Abraham and made him such an example of faith? The Bible records the answer three different times.

> Then the Lord told Abram, "Leave your country, your relatives, and your father's house, and go to the land that I will show you. . . ." So Abram departed as the Lord had instructed him. (Genesis 12:1, 4)

> Our glorious God appeared to our ancestor Abraham in Mesopotamia before he moved to Haran. God told him, "Leave your native land and your relatives, and come to the land that I will show you." So Abraham left the land of the Chaldeans and lived in Haran until his father died. (Acts 7:2-4)

> It was by faith that Abraham obeyed when God called him to leave home and go to another land that God would give him as his inheritance. He went without knowing where he was going. (Hebrews 11:8)

What set Abraham apart and made him such a remarkable example of faith? In each passage the answer is very simple: He followed when God called. No excuses. No equivocating. No hesitation. When God said to move, Abraham packed the tent! Some would call Abraham's response a blind leap of faith. But was it really? No, for two reasons.

First, *Abraham was responding to a personal encounter with God.* God first revealed himself to Abraham, and Abraham's actions were in response to God's revelation. Every time the Bible records this event, God's summons precedes Abraham's response.

Second, though Abraham may not have known his immediate destination, *he had supreme confidence in his eternal Guide.* The writer of Hebrews puts Abraham's faith in perspective. Though Abraham "did not know where he was going" as he journeyed from Mesopotamia to the land of Canaan, he saw this trip as a small part of his larger journey of faith. He could live with uncertainty and impermanence in this life "because he was confidently looking forward to a city with eternal foundations, a city designed and built by God" (Hebrews 11:10).

I thought about the importance of a guide one day as our tour bus careened around a sharp bend on a little-used road in Israel. I was leading twenty-five seminary students on a study tour, but this day was unique. Normally I guide our group, but today we had added a local Israeli guide.

Even the bus driver had not driven the roads we were now on! In fact, some of the "roads" were nothing more than dirt tracks scraped from the rocky hillside. In the politically volatile Middle East, one wrong turn could send our bus into a village where we were uninvited—and unwelcome! Our lives were in the hands of a man we had just met the previous evening. We had to trust in his ability to lead us to the promised destination.

The dirt road wound its way up the side of a mountain. On top we scrambled off the bus for a spectacular view. Walking around the top of the mountain we could see the Jordan Valley, where Abraham first crossed into the land of Canaan; the Wadi Faria he followed past Tirzah into the hill country; and the city of Shechem, with its twin peaks of Mount Ebal and Mount Gerazim, where he first settled. The guide then told us we were standing on Elon Moreh, the first location where God appeared to Abraham in the land (Genesis 12:6-7).

I had no idea what roads our bus was on or where they would lead. But I wasn't worried because the guide leading us had an excellent reputation—and he knew the way. In a slightly similar way, Abraham started on a journey before he knew the destination. But his faith was not some blind leap in the dark, because he trusted the Guide who was directing his steps.

FAITH TRUSTS WHEN GOD PROMISES

The writer of Hebrews provides a second example of Abraham's faith. God not only asked Abraham to follow him into the unknown, he also asked him to believe the impossible. Abraham was seventy-five years old when he and Sarah began their journey to the Promised Land. At a time when many men are content to sit in their rocking chairs fingering their gold watches, Abraham pulled up stakes and headed west.

But one problem remained. God not only promised

Abraham real estate, he also promised an heir. Not many seventy-five-year-old men with sixty-five-year-old wives worry about the location of the nearest elementary school when they move! Abraham must have struggled with the seeming absurdity of God's promise because he later says to God, "You have given me no children, so one of my servants will have to be my heir" (Genesis 15:3). Hey, God! It's hard to see how I will become a great nation when I won't even have any children I can call my own.

God's answer startled Abraham. "No, your servant will not be your heir, for you will have a son of your own to inherit everything I am giving you." God then took Abraham outside for an astronomy lesson. "Look up into the heavens and count the stars if you can. Your descendants will be like that—too many to count!" (15:4-5). Stock up on Pampers, Abraham, you'll soon be changing a lot of diapers!

What do you do when God makes such an outlandish statement? If you're Abraham, you trust in the truth of the statement because it was spoken by God. "And Abram believed the Lord, and the Lord declared him righteous because of his faith" (15:6). Abraham accepted God's promise, though he struggled to understand fully how it could happen.

Ten years later Abraham still struggled. He and Sarah tried to "help God" by fathering a son using Sarah's Egyptian servant girl as a surrogate mother (chapter 16). Major mistake! The resulting friction and family fighting shattered Abraham's household. Conflicts developed that continue today.

If Abraham had doubts about having children at seventy-five and tried to "help God" at eighty-six, imagine how he felt when he reached the ripe old age of ninety-nine. He and Sarah, for all practical purposes, had both passed the age when they could ever hope to have children. God chose that time to announce that a new addition would be arriving at Abraham's house in time for his one-hundredth birthday. "Regarding Sarai, your wife—her name will no longer be Sarai; from now on you will call her Sarah. And I will bless her and give you a son from her!" (17:15-16).

God's announcement stunned Abraham. "'How could I become a father at the age of one hundred?' he wondered. 'Besides, Sarah is ninety; how could she have a baby?'" (17:17). Abraham was amazed—but he immediately started calling his wife Sarah! He also obeyed God's command to practice circumcision. "On that very day Abraham took his son Ishmael and every other male in his household and circumcised them, cutting off their foreskins, exactly as God had told him" (17:23). Abraham's willingness to change his wife's name to Sarah and to circumcise everyone in his household demonstrated his trusting response to God's promise.

The writer of Hebrews highlighted Abraham's trust in God's promises—and emphasized the results. "It was by faith that Sarah together with Abraham was able to have a child, even though they were too old and Sarah was barren. Abraham believed that God would keep his promise. And so a whole nation came from this one man, Abraham, who was too old to have any children—a nation with so many people that, like the stars of the sky and the sand on the seashore, there is no way to count them" (Hebrews 11:11-12).

FAITH OBEYS WHEN GOD COMMANDS

Faith is our commitment to following when God calls and to trusting when God promises. But one essential element still might be lacking. Abraham's supreme demonstration of faith was his commitment to obeying when God commanded.

Abraham's life seemed to settle into a pattern of calm predictability. Isaac, his child of promise, was growing into a young man. The struggles with Ishmael were past. The conflicts with Canaan's kings had all been smoothed over. Life was good!

Then God threw Abraham a curveball. "Take your son, your only son—yes, Isaac, whom you love so much—and go to the land of Moriah. Sacrifice him there as a burnt offering on one of the mountains, which I will point out to you" (Genesis 22:2). *What?* Sacrifice my *son?* Do you know what you're asking? Abraham must have spent a sleepless night mulling over God's all-consuming command. God was asking him to give the supreme sacrifice: his only son, a son conceived by divine promise, a son whom he deeply loved.

But however great the personal fear, anxiety, and pain, Abraham obeyed God's command. "The next morning Abraham got up early. He saddled his donkey and took two of his servants with him, along with his son Isaac"

(22:3). By dawn's early light Abraham set out for the place selected by God as the mountain of sacrifice.

How could Abraham obey God's command without hesitation? Some would say it was because he feared the anger of a vengeful God more than he feared the loss of his son. But such a view underestimates God's love and Abraham's faith. God designed his command to test the depth of Abraham's trust and obedience. Once Abraham had demonstrated his willingness to obey God in spite of the consequences, God stopped Abraham from slaying his son. Instead, God provided a ram as a substitute. "[Abraham] took the ram and sacrificed it as a burnt offering on the altar in place of his son" (22:13). Though animal sacrifices existed from the beginning of fallen human history (4:3-5), for the first time the Bible clearly states that one life was substituted for another. God provided a substitute so Abraham would not need to sacrifice his son.

The writer of Hebrews adds one additional element that helps explain Abraham's faith. "It was by faith that Abraham offered Isaac as a sacrifice when God was testing him. Abraham, who had received God's promises, was ready to sacrifice his only son, Isaac. . . . Abraham assumed that if Isaac died, God was able to bring him back to life again. And in a sense, Abraham did receive his son back from the dead" (Hebrews 11:17, 19). What faith! Though Abraham had never seen, heard, or read of the resurrection of the dead, he reasoned that if God had predicted that Isaac was the son of promise, then God would keep his word. If God was asking Abraham to sacrifice Isaac, God would need to restore Isaac's life to fulfill his earlier promises. Abraham could obey when God asked him to do the impossible because he had supreme confidence in God's willingness and ability to keep his word.

Are you willing to obey God? If God's command seems reasonable, if it fits our plans and goals for life, and if it ultimately benefits us, then we are usually willing to obey. But what if obedience to God runs counter to our plans, hopes, and aspirations? In those times we can obey only if we have trust in the supreme power and goodness of God. Abraham was a great example of faith because he could trust God in spite of circumstances—his eyes of faith could see beyond the circumstances.

But don't put Abraham on a pedestal! His faith, remarkable though it was, is not beyond your grasp. He still struggled, just as we do, with fears, frustrations, and failures. No sooner had he arrived in the Promised Land than he abandoned it during a time of famine (Genesis 12:10. After arriving in Egypt, he lied about Sarah's being his wife because he was afraid of being killed (12:11-20). He tried to accomplish God's will through his own human effort—and he created a long-lasting family feud (16:15; 21:8-21). In the midst of his family struggles he lied a second time about Sarah being his wife (20:2-18)! Abraham struggled in his walk with God—just as you and I do.

So what set Abraham apart? Ultimately, it was his faith in God. Though he often failed, he still knew he could trust God. That sense of trust allowed Abraham to follow when God called him to a new land. It allowed Abraham to believe God's promises when they seemed so contrary to actual experience. And his faith allowed him to obey when God asked him to give up that which he held most dear.

The Father's Sacrifice

We have many tests today that seek to quantify an individual's IQ (intelligence quotient). But have you ever taken a test to determine your FQ (faith quotient)? How much do you trust God?

The supreme test of Abraham's faith was the command to give up his only son. Though God's request seemed strange (and perhaps harsh), God was asking Abraham to do nothing more than God himself had already decided to do. Before asking Abraham to part with his son, God had already decided to sacrifice his Son, Jesus Christ. "For God so loved the world that he gave his only Son, so that everyone who believes in him will not perish but have eternal life" (John 3:16).

The first—and most important—step of faith anyone can take is to trust Jesus Christ for eternal life. The Bible teaches that "all have sinned; all fall short of God's glorious standard" (Romans 3:23). Everyone has violated God's perfect standards of righteous thought and action. The Bible also says "the wages of sin is death" (6:23). God, in his perfect justice and holiness, must exclude from heaven all who fall short of his absolute standards of perfection. Anyone not sinlessly perfect receives death—physical death in this life and eternal separation from God in the lake of fire in eternity.

God's justice demands payment for sin—but God's love

wants to provide pardon, peace, and eternal life. God's solution to the dilemma was to send his perfect Son to earth to die in our place. When Jesus was on the cross he received the punishment we deserved for sin. "He was wounded and crushed for our sins. He was beaten that we might have peace. He was whipped, and we were healed! All of us have strayed away like sheep. We have left God's paths to follow our own. Yet the Lord laid on him the guilt and sins of us all" (Isaiah 53:5-6).

Was God's plan successful? Yes! The resurrection of Jesus from the dead was proof that his sacrifice was sufficient payment for our sin. "If Christ has not been raised, then your faith is useless, and you are still under condemnation for your sins. . . . But the fact is that Christ has been raised from the dead" (1 Corinthians 15:17, 20). When Jesus exploded from the tomb on that first Easter morning, he shattered death's hold on humanity and demonstrated his victory over sin and death.

Do you believe you have sinned against God? Do you believe Jesus Christ is God's Son and that he died on the cross to pay the penalty for your sins? Do you believe he rose from the dead? If so, are you willing to accept his payment for your sin and trust in him for your eternal destiny? This is the starting place for your journey of faith. God does not require you to accomplish great deeds, make great sacrifices, or experience great suffering to gain eternal life. Jesus alone has done it all. You need to believe that his actions are sufficient—and place your life in his hands. If you have never done so, perhaps you could pray a prayer like the following:

Dear Lord, I know I have done wrong and fallen short of your perfect ways. I also know and believe you sent your Son, Jesus Christ, to earth to die on the cross to pay the penalty for my sin. I now want to place my trust in Jesus Christ as the substitute for my sin. Please forgive me and give me eternal life. In Christ's name I ask this. Amen.

If you just prayed this prayer in sincerity, congratulations! You are now part of the family of God. How can you be sure? Because God said so in his Word. "And this is what God has testified: He has given us eternal life, and this life is in his Son. So whoever has God's Son has life; whoever does not have his Son does not have life. I write this to you who believe in the Son of God, so that you may know you have eternal life" (1 John 5:11-13).

Trust and Obey

If you have placed your trust in Jesus Christ as your personal Savior, what's next? Having trusted in Christ for our eternal destiny, we must now learn to trust him for our day-to-day needs. Abraham can be our example. His life of faith involved following God's directions, believing God's words, and obeying God's commands. You can do the same.

Our Christian life starts with trust. Believe God, accept what he has said, and trust in his goodness. That faith then allows us to follow his directions, believe his Word, and obey his commands. We must first trust, then obey. Over a century ago, John Sammis wrote a song that captures this order for our lives. The song is aptly entitled "Trust and Obey."

When we walk with the Lord in the light of his Word
What a glory He sheds on our way!
While we do His good will, He abides with us still,
And with all who will trust and obey.

But we never can prove the delights of His love
Until all on the altar we lay;
For the favor He shows, and the joy He bestows,
Are for them who will trust and obey.

Chorus:
Trust and obey, for there's no other way
To be happy in Jesus, but to trust and obey.

Questions to Ponder

Faith is more than just intellectual assent, more than just believing a set of facts. It's an active trust in God and his Word.

1. Have you placed your trust for eternal life in Jesus Christ and his death on your behalf? If you just made this decision, find a church that believes and teaches the Bible—and tell the pastor what you have done.
2. In what areas do you struggle most to trust God?
3. Make a list of the specific ways you have seen God work in your life. Keep the list nearby, and read through it whenever you struggle with doubt. Remembering what he has done for you in the past will help you trust him for the future.

4. Memorize Hebrews 11:1, and ask God to help you grow stronger in your faith.

It is impossible to please God without faith. Anyone who wants to come to him must believe that there is a God and that he rewards those who sincerely seek him. (Hebrews 11:6)

7

FAITHFULNESS

Can God Depend on Me?

It Keeps Going, and Going . . .

Dependability sells! Three decades ago Timex sold watches on live national television by focusing on dependability. The announcer would do something outrageous like strap the watch to the propeller of an outboard motor and run the engine in a tank of water. He would then stop the engine, remove the watch, and hold it up for the camera. As the audience watched the second hand sweep around the dial, the announcer delivered the punch line. "Timex! Takes a licking and keeps on ticking!" In the unpredictable days of live television, this stunt spoke volumes about the faith the company had in the watch's dependability. "Buy me!" the advertisement screamed. "I won't let you down."

Dependability still sells. The lonely Maytag repairman, with his clean uniform and sad expression, reinforces the message that Maytag is produced by "the dependability people." Your Maytag appliance won't let you down.

But the darling of dependability in advertising today has to be the ubiquitous Energizer bunny. It keeps going, and going, and going—outpacing marathoners and out-lasting everyone from Darth Vader to Santa Claus. With every beat of the drum this fuzzy pink rabbit reminds viewers that its batteries last longer. Your Energizer batteries won't let you down.

If only real life matched the ads!

Our First Car

I can recall in vivid detail the first new car my wife and I bought. Actually, it wasn't really *new*. It was a dealer demonstrator, and the odometer read less than twelve thousand miles when we bought it. It looked great! Before buying the car we watched television ads that stressed its innovative features and solid construction. I'll not share the name of the manufacturer—but I will tell you about "the car from hell"!

I began having my doubts about the car when the hood, trunk, and roof started turning a lighter shade of red than the doors and fenders. The car developed the automotive equivalent of male-pattern baldness. But the real crisis began during rush hour in Harrisburg, Pennsylvania, in the middle of a blizzard.

I was in Pennsylvania to attend a funeral. On my way home, the car just stopped in the middle of downtown Harrisburg. Died! Quit! Conked out! Sleet mixed with snow pelted my face as I got out of the car and looked under the hood. Battery? OK. Spark plugs and wires? OK. Carburetor? OK. Phone nearby to call AAA? No! I climbed back into the car with the hood up, waiting for a policeman to come by and rescue me. Out of frustration I turned the key one last time. The motor sprang to life as if nothing were wrong! And that was just the beginning. . . .

Over the next year that car took on a mind of its own. Day or night. Wet or dry. Summer or winter. Cold or hot. Superhighway or country road. In no predictable pattern and for no detectable reason the car would periodically just stop running.

I know what you're thinking: Why didn't we take the car to a dealership to have it fixed? We did. Many times. We changed the computer module—twice! We discovered a recall for a part in the engine and had it replaced. No change. (One problem, naturally, was that the car would never act up at the dealership.)

Once we were driving to a store when the car began to sputter. We were only a few miles from the dealership, so I did a quick U-turn and headed in that direction. Now they would have to find the problem! But the closer I got to the dealership, the less the car shook. With the garage in sight the last bit of hesitation disappeared and the car purred smoothly. Rats!

Finally I couldn't take it anymore. I'm not a skilled mechanic (today's politically correct society would classify me as "mechanically challenged"), but even I could tell the problem was electrical. The solution? Replace every electrical part possible. So, armed with a new coil, distributor cap, spark-plug wires, and spark plugs, I attacked the problem.

Opening the box with the coil, I found a small notice saying the new coil may not look like the original because it had been modified to correct a potential problem. *Aha!* Then I opened the box with the new distributor cap. Inside was a small notice saying the distributor cap may not look like the original because it had been modified to correct a potential problem. *Aha* a second time!

After many trips to the dealership, hundreds of dollars in "expert" repairs, and countless hours sitting beside the road waiting for the car to restart, I had finally solved the problem. Two defective parts had allowed moisture to collect and temporarily disrupt the electrical system. We sold that car a few months later, and we have never owned another car made by that company! Dependability is important!

How Important Is Faithfulness?

I remember when I joined the Boy Scouts. The troop met in the community room at the local volunteer fire company. My friends and I rode there together for our meetings. As new Boy Scouts we had to memorize the Boy Scout motto, pledge, and other slogans. One began, "A scout is trustworthy, loyal. . . ." I find it amazing that those simple words made such a profound impact on my life. I can still recite them from memory.

Trustworthy. Faithful. Dependable. Loyal. All of these are different facets of the same character trait. How good are we at sticking to commitments, promises, and relationships we have made? Are we dependable?

Society today values faithfulness and dependability as

good ideals, but most don't expect to find them. In the past, manufacturers sought to develop "brand loyalty" among their customers—loyalty that passed from generation to generation. "My father drove a Plymouth. I drive a Plymouth. And my son will drive a Plymouth." But brand loyalty has gone the way of the Nash, Hudson, Henry J, and Studebaker. Today we change brands almost as often as we change clothes. Why? Some of the reasons have to do with dependability.

Brand loyalty is a two-way street. Many manufacturers started cutting corners and cheapening products to save money. At the same time, they inflated claims in their advertising and pitched products that could never meet the expectations they created. After spending thousands of dollars to purchase "precision driving machines," customers fumed for countless hours in dealership waiting rooms while their cars had parts replaced in recalls. It's hard to remain loyal to a particular brand or company when you feel ripped off.

A lack of faithfulness in the marketplace might be a sign of healthy competition and free-market economics, but unfortunately the same attitude has crept into our homes and families. And there it produces misery, anger, and pain. We have replaced "till death do us part" with prenuptial agreements. Extramarital affairs, once the scandal of Hollywood, are now old news in most small towns. We hardly raise an eyebrow when we hear of still another individual caught in such an affair.

I grew up in a community where marriage and faithfulness were the norm. *All* my friends came from two-parent homes. We were shocked when one of my friend's parents went through a divorce. It was rare—and traumatic. Today divorce is regarded by many as no big deal. Incompatibility. Irreconcilable differences. No-fault divorce. For some, marriage is no larger a commitment than choosing a job or buying a home. You hope it will work out, but if it doesn't—oh well.

The church fares little better than the home. God ordained the local church to be a gathering of the faithful. In an earlier generation, members of a local congregation made a commitment to God and to each other to be the visible representation of God's light to their community. Commitment to a local congregation was synonymous with commitment to the Lord. "Church hopping" was a rarity, if it happened at all.

Today, many Christians shop for churches the same way they shop for cars. Which is the most stylish? the biggest? the one with the most features? the most powerful? People "test-drive" the worship service and see what other "options" the church has to offer. Churches must "market" themselves to attract and hold potential "customers." But churches that cater to what the "customers" *want* to hear can seldom afford to share with those people the message they desperately *need* to hear.

So how important is faithfulness? Pick up your newspaper and see how many tragic headlines can be traced to a lack of faithfulness. Today's *Dallas Morning News* reported further details on the treasonous actions of a government employee and the damage to the national security of the United States caused by his betrayal. Nine individuals died because of his willingness to sell out America. Another article described the court case of a husband who brutally shot his wife in the legs because he was embarrassed that she had a job while he did not. She had to have both legs amputated because his pride was more important to him than her well-being. A jury convicted a politician of demanding and receiving bribes while in office. He peddled public contracts for personal gain.

Faithfulness. Dependability. Trustworthiness. Everyone values it; few practice it consistently. Yet models of faithfulness *do* exist. Many live lives of faithful obscurity—their reliability taken for granted. Others have demonstrated faithfulness while in the public eye. Billy Graham has always been one of my personal heroes. A lifetime of service without a hint of financial or sexual impropriety.

Another modern hero of mine is Chuck Swindoll, with whom I am privileged to work at Dallas Theological Seminary. Gifted speaker. Talented writer. Fun-loving, Harley-riding leader. But more than all that, he is a man of faithfulness. Faithfulness to God. Faithfulness to his wife, Cynthia, and their children. Faithfulness to the ministries he leads. Faithfulness to those who work beside him in ministry.

In November 1994, I flew to Pennsylvania because of a family emergency. My dad was scheduled to undergo heart-bypass surgery. I know bypass surgery is becoming quite common. I know it's almost considered routine. All those things are true—unless it's *your* father being wheeled to surgery on the gurney. Then it's neither common nor routine.

The hours dragged by as we waited for the doctor to tell us how the operation had gone. Even after Dad came out of surgery, we spent several more days waiting for those precious few moments each hour when we could enter the cardiac-care unit to be with him.

During one visitation period in the cardiac-care unit, the nurse called me aside and excitedly announced that my physician from Dallas had called to check on my dad's progress and recovery. My physician? "Yes," she said, "Dr. Swindoll!"

Dad recovered, and I flew back to Dallas. On my desk was a handwritten note from Chuck that read, in part, "You have been through a long and lonely journey these past several days. I understand. I've been there with my dad. So many, many times you have come to my mind. Each time I've sent a word upward. . . . What a great feeling is relief! With a smile that says, 'Welcome back.'" I treasure that note, and I deeply appreciate Chuck's faithfulness in writing it.

So how can we become more faithful? What secrets can the Bible share to help us develop lives characterized by faithfulness? Two experienced military veterans, Joshua and Caleb, can supply us with some answers.

Hangin' with Moses

Faithfulness begins in small areas. Joshua stepped onto the pages of Bible history to lead a party of warriors against a group of nomadic raiders. These nomads, the Amalekites, attacked the Israelites in the wilderness. Most likely they were raiding those families unfortunate enough to be living on the outskirts of the camp of Israel. The Amalekites needed to be stopped, and Moses put Joshua in charge of the commandos.

Though the whole account of the battle with the Amalekites takes only nine verses (Exodus 17:8-16), the Bible makes two crucial observations about Joshua. First, he faithfully executed Moses' orders. "Joshua *did what Moses had commanded.* He led his men out to fight the army of Amalek" (17:10, italics added). Why add this phrase? Perhaps to set Joshua apart from the rest of the people. Just a few verses earlier the people had "grumbled and complained to Moses" (17:2-3). Second, Joshua completed the assignment. "Joshua and his troops were able to crush the army of Amalek" (17:13). The children of Israel were whiners; Joshua was a winner.

Moses found in Joshua someone he could trust to obey orders and to follow the job through to completion. The battle was over in just one day—the entire encounter nothing more than a brief footnote in the account of the amazing events that took place during those forty years in the wilderness. Yet Joshua's faithfulness this one day changed his life forever.

Moses found the task of governing Israel to be more than he could handle. His father-in-law, Jethro, saw the strain and suggested Moses appoint judges for the people to assist in leadership (chapter 18). Moses followed Jethro's advice. Perhaps Jethro's wise counsel also encouraged Moses to make other changes. We cannot be sure, but when Joshua next appears in the Bible he has received a promotion. "So Moses and his assistant Joshua climbed up the mountain of God" (24:13). Moses made Joshua his assistant. When Moses went up Mount Sinai to meet with God, Joshua walked beside him. What a promotion!

Faithfulness doesn't just happen. Faithfulness in small areas will usually lead to greater trust and responsibility. Jesus shared the parable of the man who went on a long journey and entrusted ten servants with ten *minas*. A mina was the equivalent of just over one pound of silver. It could be further divided into one hundred *drachmas*—each drachma being the average wage someone received for a day's work. The man gave each servant approximately three months' salary—a small, but still significant, responsibility.

When the man returned as king, he summoned each servant and asked for a report. "The first servant reported a tremendous gain—ten times as much as the original amount! 'Well done!' the king exclaimed. 'You are a trustworthy servant. You have been faithful with the little I entrusted to you, so you will be governor of ten cities as your reward'" (Luke 19:16-17). Wow! Faithfulness over three months' salary brought far greater reward—and responsibility.

Moses gave Joshua a single task. Not large. Not difficult. Not complex. But his ability to obey and to stick with the task until its completion demonstrated his faithfulness. Later, when Moses looked for a personal aide, Joshua was the one chosen.

What responsibilities do you have today? How faithful have you been? No job should be too small or insignificant. "Work with enthusiasm, as though you were working for the Lord rather than for people. Remember that the Lord will reward each one of us for the good we do" (Ephesians 6:7-8).

The Mossad's First Mission

The Mossad is modern Israel's crack intelligence organization—Israel's version of America's CIA. This group of supersleuths has tracked down escaped Nazis and political terrorists. They have also pulled off some of the most dangerous and daring undercover operations in history—and we only know a fraction of the things they have done!

Even today's Mossad would be proud of their nation's first spy mission, undertaken over 3,400 years before the modern state of Israel came into existence! The children of Israel stood on the edge of the land promised them by God. But this new nation knew little about the land they were about to invade. Moses chose twelve spies to explore the new land, and he issued specific instructions (Numbers 13:17-20):

- "See what the land is like and find out whether the people living there are strong or weak, few or many." (Check out the opposition!)
- "What kind of land do they live in? Is it good or bad?" (Check out the terrain!)
- "Do their towns have walls or are they unprotected?" (Check out the defenses!)
- "How is the soil? Is it fertile or poor?" (Check out the productivity!)
- "Are there many trees?" (Check out the potential!)

And whom did Moses select for this elite group of spies? "Hoshea son of Nun" (13:8). What? Who's Hoshea? I thought you were talking about Joshua! Be patient— Moses explains who this is a few verses later. "By this time Moses had changed Hoshea's name to Joshua" (13:16). Evidently, Joshua's original name was Hoshea ("salvation"). Moses changed it (possibly after the victory over the Amalekites) to Joshua ("the Lord is salvation"). The Bible provides the names of all twelve spies, but only one is singled out in this fashion. Joshua was the spy with the new name—a name that focused attention on the Lord.

The spies returned with their report. All agreed the land was fertile and productive. "It is indeed a magnificent country—a land flowing with milk and honey. Here is some of its fruit as proof" (13:27). But the spies could not agree on their evaluation of the people of the land. Ten of the spies issued a majority report—and it wasn't good news (13:28):

- "The people living there are powerful." (They are too strong!)
- "Their cities and towns are fortified and very large." (They are too well defended!)
- "We also saw the descendants of Anak [i.e., giants] who are living there!" (They are too big!)

Two spies—Joshua and Caleb—stood and challenged the majority report. They didn't see obstacles; they saw opportunities. Caleb spoke first: "'Let's go at once to take the land,' he said. 'We can certainly conquer it!'" (13:30). When the people refused to listen, both Joshua and Caleb stressed the wonderful opportunity being rejected. "The land we explored is a wonderful land!" (14:7). How could these two see the land and people so differently than the other ten spies?

Joshua and Caleb's secret was their ability to view all possible problems from God's perspective. Problem #1: This "good land" is populated by powerful people, some of whom are giants. Answer: "Don't be afraid of the people of the land. They are only helpless prey to us!" (14:9). I like the poetic nature of the King James translation here: "They are bread for us." We'll eat 'em up! Problem #2: These powerful people live in large, fortified cities. Answer: "They have no protection, but the Lord is with us! Don't be afraid of them!" (14:9).

Joshua and Caleb did not walk through Canaan wearing rose-colored glasses. They saw the same problems, but they saw them through God's eyes. Physical giants are no threat when God is on our side. High walls and thick gates are no barrier when God removes their protection. The real threat to Israel was not the people of Canaan or their defenses. The most serious threat was the temptation to abandon God. Joshua and Caleb started and ended their speech in Numbers 14:9 with a warning: "Do not rebel against the Lord. . . . Don't be afraid of them!"

The final vote wasn't even close. When the 603,550 men of fighting age made their decision on which report to accept, Joshua and Caleb lost in a landslide—603,548 voted for the majority report! Joshua and Caleb had *no* support. Peer pressure is something all of us have faced at some point in our life. We all know how difficult it is to stand out in a crowd. Imagine the pressure on Joshua and Caleb! No one from their tribes or clans or even their immediate families stood with them. How were they able to do it?

Caleb's Secret

Caleb in Hebrew means "dog," and Caleb certainly had the tenacity of a bulldog. He shared his secret for faithfulness when he appeared before Joshua after the forty-year period of wandering in the wilderness to ask for his inheritance in the land. What kept Caleb faithful? Conviction, commitment, and confidence.

CONVICTION

Caleb could stand alone with Joshua because he had given Moses a truthful appraisal. Years later, Caleb would recall, "I returned and gave from my heart a good report" (Joshua 14:7). He could stand alone because he knew what he was standing for. He had a deep, abiding belief in what he knew to be true, and he was willing to take a stand for what was right.

Martin Luther's name is synonymous with the Protestant Reformation. This German priest challenged the Roman Church and changed the course of church history. He stood for his convictions, based on the Word of God. At the Diet of Worms, Luther appeared before German princes, nobles, and clergy. They demanded he retract his teachings—and everyone understood the implied penalty for disobedience. Luther stood and responded. "Unless I am refuted and convicted by testimonies of the Scriptures or by clear arguments . . . my conscience is bound in the

Word of God. I cannot and will not recant anything." He stood by his convictions.

COMMITMENT

Knowing the truth of what you believe is one thing. Being willing to stand by those beliefs is another. Caleb saw the tide turn against his convictions. The crowd didn't buy his arguments. Wasn't this the time for compromise, acquiescence, reconsideration? Not for Caleb! "For my part, I followed the Lord my God completely" (Joshua 14:8). If God was bigger than the giants in the land, he was also bigger than the disbelieving Israelites in the wilderness. Caleb cast his lot with God.

Modern society discounts conviction and commitment. Believe in something too strongly and society labels you a "fundamentalist." Commit to something too wholeheartedly and they call you a fanatic or an extremist. Words are powerful tools to shape and mold thoughts and beliefs— and labels are often used as verbal cattle prods to force someone to conform and submit. In an age that promotes freedom, diversity, and tolerance, society shows little tolerance for those who commit to God and his Word. Commitment may be unpopular, but it's an essential ingredient of faithfulness.

CONFIDENCE

Faithfulness is a by-product of faith. I can be faithful to God if I'm absolutely sure he will do what he has promised. Caleb was faithful because he had complete confidence in God—and that confidence came from experience. God promised Joshua and Caleb he would keep them alive in the wilderness and allow them to enter the Promised Land. Forty years of wandering in the wilderness was followed by five years of active warfare as Israel fought to take the land. So what became of God's promise? "Now, as you can see, the Lord has kept me alive and well as he promised for all these forty-five years since Moses made this promise. . . . Today I am eighty-five years old. I am as strong now as I was when Moses sent me on that journey, and I can still travel and fight as well as I could then" (Joshua 14:10-11).

Caleb's confidence came from watching God work. The God who had helped him in the past could be trusted for the future. He was so confident that he went to Joshua with a bold request. "I'm asking you to give me the hill country that the Lord promised me. You will remember that as scouts we found the Anakites [the giants!] living there in great, walled cities. But if the Lord is with me, I will drive them out of the land, just as the Lord said" (14:12). At the age of eighty-five, Caleb wasn't ready to retire. He wanted a piece of the action! And he didn't want anything too easy. He wanted the hills with the largest giants and the strongest cities! God hadn't changed, and Caleb was as confident of the outcome now as he had been forty-five years earlier! The bigger they are, the harder they'll fall!

Commander in Chief

Turning back to Joshua for a moment, we find him facing the greatest challenge of his life. For forty years Joshua had served as second in command to Moses. Great guy! Wonderful commander! Fabulous assistant! But could he *replace* Moses? I'm sure some in Israel had their doubts. It's hard following a legend like Moses, who led so powerfully for so long. The book of Deuteronomy ends with a suitable epitaph that captures the essence of Moses' leadership: "There has never been another prophet like Moses, whom the Lord knew face to face. . . . It was through Moses that the Lord demonstrated his mighty power and terrifying acts in the sight of all Israel" (Deuteronomy 34:10, 12). Joshua was prepared to conquer the physical giants in the land, but how could he hope to replace a spiritual giant like Moses?

God appeared to Joshua with the answer. Three times he urged Joshua to "be strong and courageous" (Joshua 1:6, 7, 9). Joshua, like Caleb, had to develop conviction, commitment, and confidence. Each element was as essential to Joshua's faithfulness as it was to Caleb's.

CONVICTION

Joshua had to be convinced that he was God's choice to lead Israel. Though he did not possess the unique personality of Moses, he had to realize that God would supply the needed ability to lead. "Now Joshua son of Nun was full of the spirit of wisdom, for Moses had laid his hands on him" (Deuteronomy 34:9). Spiritual leadership is dependent on God's spiritual enablement, not on natural ability. Israel needed Moses in the wilderness, but they needed Joshua for the conquest. God wanted to convince Joshua of this, so he said, "Be strong and courageous, for you will lead my people to possess all the land" (Joshua 1:6). Joshua was God's choice.

COMMITMENT

Conviction alone wasn't enough to guarantee faithfulness. Conviction had to be followed by personal commitment. God reminded Joshua of his need to know and obey the Word of God. God would measure Joshua's success as a leader by his commitment to God's Word. "Be strong and very courageous. Obey all the laws Moses gave you. *Do not turn away from them,* and you will be successful in everything you do. Study this Book of the Law continually. Meditate on it day and night so you may be sure to obey all that is written in it. Only then will you succeed" (Joshua 1:7-8, italics added).

Joshua may personally have felt inadequate as a leader, but he had to develop the conviction that God had called him to replace Moses. God would give him the ability to be an effective leader, but those convictions called for commitment. To be an effective leader, Joshua needed to master the ability to submit to the heavenly King and wholeheartedly obey him.

A few chapters later, God reminded Joshua of the necessity of this commitment. Just after crossing the Jordan River, Joshua prepared to begin his conquest of the land. Jericho loomed as the first major obstacle. Camped just a few miles from this walled fortress, Joshua felt the full weight of his position as commander in chief. What if the city proved too difficult to conquer? What if the people of the land were better warriors? What if the toll in human life proved to be too great?

Whatever Joshua was thinking, his thoughts were interrupted when he looked up to see a man standing in front of him with a drawn sword. Something didn't seem right. Joshua didn't recognize him, so he asked, "Are you friend or foe?" (5:13). The warrior's answer startled him. "'Neither one,' he replied. 'I am commander of the Lord's army'" (5:14). God had not promised unswerving allegiance to Israel; he had called on Israel to promise unswerving allegiance to him. God's forces could fight for Israel—or against Israel.

God's commander was in Israel's midst, watching for signs of obedience and commitment. Joshua immediately fell facedown and humbly asked this heavenly Commander, "What do you want your servant to do?" (5:14). The burdens and problems of leadership now fell into proper focus. The battle belonged to God, not Joshua. God was in charge, and Joshua was to be the committed servant.

But Joshua still needed one final element to help him develop faithfulness—an absolute sense of confidence that would take him through the battles ahead.

CONFIDENCE

God often tests commitment in the crucible of conflict. It's easy to commit to God when manna shows up on the ground each morning and God is appearing to you in visions. It's harder to have confidence when the wheels come off and God seems to be silent. Joshua had to gear himself up for the hard times ahead. God's solution was to reaffirm his protection. "Be strong and courageous! Do not be afraid or discouraged. For the Lord your God is with you wherever you go" (Joshua 1:9).

Did Joshua remain confident? At Jericho Joshua ordered the people, "Shout! For the Lord has given you the city!" (6:16). The outcome was never in doubt. Joshua led Israel in victorious conquest because he *knew* God would give victory. Later Joshua ordered the heavens to halt their movement on Israel's behalf. "Joshua prayed to the Lord in front of all the people of Israel. He said, 'Let the sun stand still over Gibeon, and the moon over the valley of Aijalon'" (10:12). That's confidence! He knew God would do what he had promised.

As for Me and My Family

Society idolizes the strength and beauty of youth, but true wisdom belongs to those who have mastered life and its secrets. The next generation of Israelite leaders was busy developing their new land when they received a summons to appear at Shechem. Over twenty years had passed since Joshua had led Israel in conquest and divided the land among the tribes. Joshua, the seasoned sage, was summoning Israel's new leaders for one last meeting before his impending death. What final words of wisdom would this battle-hardened veteran give to the next generation?

It's no surprise that the man whose life epitomized faithful service for God focused on the subject of faithfulness. After reviewing all God had done for the nation, Joshua called the leaders to action. "So honor the Lord and serve him wholeheartedly" (Joshua 24:14). Steadfast commitment to God remained the main theme of Joshua's life.

This elder statesman had no illusions about the temptations facing the fledgling nation. He had lived long enough to see an entire generation reject the Lord and perish in the wilderness. He had watched good soldiers die because of one soldier's sin at Jericho. The temptation to turn from the Lord was great, and the consequences would be catastrophic.

Joshua laid the issue on the line with this gathering of leaders. "If you are unwilling to serve the Lord, then choose today whom you will serve. . . . But as for me and my family, we will serve the Lord" (24:15). Joshua planned to end his life the way he had always lived it—in faithful service to God. And he challenged the next generation to tread the same path.

Joshua was also wise enough to know how easy it would be for Israel to forget his words. The next generation needed something to remind them of this important commitment. This wise leader first recorded the words lest they be lost. "So Joshua made a covenant with the people that day at Shechem, committing them to a permanent and binding contract between themselves and the Lord. Joshua recorded these things in the Book of the Law of God" (24:25-26). Memories might fail, so Joshua preserved the words.

Joshua then erected a permanent reminder of the commitment the people had made. "As a reminder of their agreement, he took a huge stone and rolled it beneath the oak tree beside the Tabernacle of the Lord. Joshua said to all the people, 'This stone has heard everything the Lord said to us. It will be a witness to testify against you if you go back on your word to God'" (24:26-27). Stones. Visible reminders of God's past faithfulness and the people's commitment. From the Jordan River to Shechem, Joshua repeatedly set up reminders to help the people call to mind God's past work and their ongoing commitment (4:1-9; 7:26; 8:28-29, 32; 10:27; 22:24-28; 24:26). Maybe we need more piles of stones in our lives today!

Joshua and Caleb. Two men from different family backgrounds. Men who assumed different levels of responsibility during Israel's wanderings in the wilderness and during the conquest of Canaan. Yet two men who shared the characteristic of faithfulness to their God—whose lives ran counter to an entire generation.

In the great celestial arena, Joshua and Caleb must surely have box seats from which to watch today's race of the faithful. They must be part of the "huge crowd of witnesses" that surrounds us as we "run with endurance the race that God has set before us" (Hebrews 12:1). They are cheering us on with their own testimonies of faithfulness to God. And they are pointing to the supreme example of faithfulness—Jesus Christ. "Think about all he endured when sinful people did such terrible things to him, so that you don't become weary and give up" (12:3).

Jesus faithfully followed his heavenly Father's commands, even submitting to death on the cross. "My Father! If it is possible, let this cup of suffering be taken away from me. Yet I want your will, not mine" (Matthew 26:39). Caleb and Joshua faithfully followed God, even when it required them to stand against their own families and friends. And now God asks you to make the same commitment. Are you ready, and willing, to repeat after Joshua, "Choose today whom you will serve. . . . But as for me and my family, we will serve the Lord"? Why not make that commitment right now?

Questions to Ponder

Faithfulness is our commitment to remain true to God whatever the circumstances. Several elements characterize an individual who is faithful.

1. Faithfulness begins with strong convictions. Do you know what you believe, based on the teaching of God's Word? Do you attend a local church, Sunday school class, or Bible study where you are able to learn what God's Word really says?

2. Faithfulness follows commitment. Are you willing to commit to following God and obeying him? Write out your commitment on a piece of paper, and put it in your Bible as a reminder. Or better yet, write your commitment in your Bible, sign it, and date it. This can be your physical reminder—your "huge stone" (Joshua 24:26) set up to keep you from forgetting your commitment to follow God.

3. Faithfulness allows us to stay true to God because we maintain confidence in him. Make a list of the ways God has met your physical, spiritual, and emotional needs over the past year. Be specific.

Keep a prayer journal to chronicle the ways God has been working in your life.

4. Memorize Joshua 24:15, and ask God to help make those words the passion of your life.

Never let loyalty and kindness get away from you! Wear them like a necklace; write them deep within your heart. Then you will find favor with both God and people, and you will gain a good reputation. (Proverbs 3:3-4)

8

BALANCE

*Does All Work and No Play
Make Jack a Dull Boy?*

Out of Balance

I started out in Dallas in the banking business. No, I wasn't
related to J. R. Ewing. And I wasn't in top management.
My first job in Dallas was part-time teller at the drive-in
window of a small local bank. The bank opened in July
1974, and my wife and I blew into town a month later.
They needed part-time help. And as a new seminary
student, I needed a job!

Every weekday (except holidays!) I sat at my window
overseeing two drive-in lanes. Most afternoons were predictable. But I dreaded Fridays—and the fifteenth and last
day of each month. Those were the high-volume days
when lines of cars would stretch back to the street. And if
the fifteenth or the last day of the month fell *on* Friday, the
workers cashing paychecks, stores making deposits, and
individuals getting money for the weekend overwhelmed
me. Chaos! Bedlam! Total confusion!

But the worst moment of all on those days came when
we closed the bank and "balanced out" for the day. The

process seemed simple enough. Start with the opening balance in my cash drawer. Add the slips for cash deposits. Subtract the checks and slips for cash withdrawals—and pray that the closing balance matched the actual amount of money remaining! If the drawer was "out of balance," I was forced to go back and check every transaction to see if the slips matched each cash deposit and withdrawal. A laborious, but necessary, process!

Balance benefits more than bank tellers. It's essential for living life successfully. Balance is the ability to hold everything in harmony—to keep differing elements in a state of equilibrium. We don't think much about balance until something goes wrong that throws our lives into disarray.

- While reconciling your checkbook with your monthly bank statement you realize that you forgot to enter a check for $150—and your checkbook has been *out of balance.*
- You begin an exercise program but develop severe cramping while working out. A blood test shows that a chemical *imbalance*—a potassium deficiency—caused the cramping.
- Your car steering wheel shakes and vibrates as you drive. A mechanic identifies the problem—your tires are *out of balance.*
- You awaken in the morning. But as you stand up, a wave of dizziness and nausea overwhelms you, forcing you back into bed. You call your doctor,

who suspects that an inner-ear infection is
throwing off your *sense of balance.*

Living the successful Christian life requires balance.
Solomon, the wise king who, unfortunately, lived much of
his life out of balance, concluded in the end: "There is a
time for everything, a season for every activity under
heaven" (Ecclesiastes 3:1). The difficulty is discovering
God's balance.

Without a sense of balance some Christians *burn out*
from overactivity while others *rust out* from lack of involvement. Still others *foul out* from wrong decisions and
bad choices. In any case, you're out! Jesus recognized—and
taught—the importance of balance.

On one particular occasion Jesus sent the twelve disciples on a vital mission throughout Israel (Mark 6:7-13).
They preached, cast out demons, and performed miraculous healings. When they came back to Jesus, they were
wild with success, brimming over with enthusiasm.
Crowds followed them back to the Master! Pandemonium
prevailed as the masses packed ever more closely around
Jesus and his disciples.

And then Jesus said, "Let's get away from the crowds for
a while and rest" (6:31). I picture the disciples rolling their
eyes in disbelief. *What?* Leave when the excitement is just
beginning to build? The discipleship business is booming!
We can't stop now! They were too preoccupied with ministry, and they needed a lesson in balance. Too much
busyness—even when it's busyness on behalf of God—can
be harmful.

What is the secret for maintaining balance? How can we keep our lives from spinning out of control? Perhaps we can find some answers in a home Jesus visited on numerous occasions—the home of Mary, Martha, and Lazarus in the village of Bethany. We are invited into their home on three separate occasions in the Bible. And each visit is instructive.

Too Busy to Spend Time with God

As Jesus and his disciples traveled through Israel, they relied on friends and followers to supply food and lodging. Ordinary individuals opened their homes to show hospitality to the Son of God. Most remain anonymous, but one special family is identified by name. Perhaps it's because their location near Jerusalem made their home a particular favorite. Perhaps it's because of the close-knit bond that developed between the two sisters, their brother, and the Lord. Or perhaps it's because of the unique events that took place as Jesus interacted with this family. But for whatever reason, the home of Mary and Martha took on special significance in the life of our Lord.

The village of Bethany sits on the eastern slope of the Mount of Olives, just two miles from Jerusalem. Though Jews from the northern part of the country could travel directly south from Galilee to Jerusalem through Samaria, many chose to bypass that region because of the animosity between the Jews and the Samaritans. Thus many Jews took a more roundabout road to Jerusalem that led them down the eastern side of the Jordan Valley toward the Dead Sea. Those travelers would then cross the Jordan near Jericho and make the long, winding journey up from Jericho to Jerusalem through the Judean wilderness. After a steep climb through this forbidding land, they would see the Mount of Olives rising up as the last obstacle to Jerusalem. It made a logical resting place after the day-long journey from Jericho.

Jesus and his disciples used both roadways to travel to and from Jerusalem. On one occasion Jesus "had to go through Samaria" because of a divine appointment with a woman at a well (John 4:4). But on other occasions Jesus traveled through Jericho on his way to Jerusalem (Matthew 20:29). His friends and followers who lived along the different roads had no way of knowing if—or when—Jesus and his disciples might stop to seek lodging.

The Gospel of Luke presents every hostess's nightmare. Friends dropping by without notice. Uninvited! Unexpected! Unannounced! But not unwelcome. "As Jesus and the disciples continued on their way to Jerusalem, they came to a village where a woman named Martha welcomed them into her home" (Luke 10:38). She would have done her modern-day namesake Martha Stewart proud!

Picture the scene. No sooner had Jesus and the disciples walked through the door than Martha sprang into action. Someone needs to go to the cistern to draw more water to wash their feet. But what about the evening meal? Extra grain must be ground for bread. Wait! Before grinding the grain, I'll need still more water to prepare the dough. Stop! Before I prepare the dough, the fire should be burning in the oven. Oh no! We're almost out of firewood. Someone needs to collect extra firewood before we start the fire. Hold it! We don't have enough fruit or vegetables to feed all the guests. Someone needs to go to the market to buy the necessary produce.

Martha's mind went into overdrive. "Martha was worrying over the big dinner she was preparing" (10:40). Don't judge Martha too harshly. Hospitality was an important part of ancient Near Eastern culture, and Martha was serving Israel's Messiah. My wife sometimes reminds me that if it weren't for the Marthas of the world, nothing would ever get done. Martha, the conscientious older sister, was responsible for running the household, and she took her job seriously.

But Martha was not the only woman in the house. She had a younger sister, Mary. While Martha ran around drawing water, washing, grinding, kneading, baking, peeling—and panting—Mary "sat at the Lord's feet, listening to what he taught" (10:39). Oblivious to the whirlwind of activity taking place around her, Mary sat quietly, soaking in the words of her Lord.

I suspect Martha first tried some "subtle" ways to get Mary's attention. A few glares in Mary's direction. A few clicks of her tongue. Some clearing of her throat—loudly! But it was all in vain. Mary remained planted at the Lord's feet, her eyes glued to his face. She listened so intently to the Lord that she never noticed her sister's preparations or her rising level of frustration.

Martha finally chose a more direct course of action. If Mary listened so intently to Jesus, then Martha would get Jesus to set her straight. And besides, Jesus should have noticed that Mary wasn't acting as a proper hostess. So Martha stormed up to Jesus and said, "Lord, doesn't it seem unfair to you that my sister just sits here while I do all the work? Tell her to come and help me" (10:40). Bam! Martha had the subtlety of a two-by-four.

Jesus' response certainly raised some eyebrows in a society that expected men to sit around and discuss weighty issues while women did housework. "My dear Martha, you are so upset over all these details! There is really only one thing worth being concerned about. Mary has discovered it—and I won't take it away from her" (10:41-42). Martha was so upset about the details that she missed the big picture! Jesus was in her house teaching, and she was too busy counting cups to pay attention.

Unfortunately, we often miss the point of this story. Our response goes something like this: *Boy! If Jesus ever came to my house, I wouldn't worry about fixing dinner. I'd call Domino's or Little Caesar's and sit at his feet till the pizza arrived!* But Jesus had more in mind than dinner.

Everything Martha was doing was good and proper. Her problem was that she focused so much on these details that she lost her perspective. She wanted to prepare a feast when a simple meal would have sufficed. She worried about drawing water from the cistern while the Fountain of Living Water sat in the next room. She fretted over preparing enough bread while the Bread of Life lodged in her house. She concentrated on the trees—and missed the forest.

Our society fosters the "Martha syndrome." We reward

diligence and applaud activity. We crave "labor-saving devices" to give us more free time. But then we use those devices to cram even more activity into each twenty-four-hour period. Speed dialing. Cellular phones. Pagers. Fax machines. Computers. *Headline News.* In the midst of our activity, like Martha, we become "so upset over all these details."

Are you too busy to pray and read your Bible? How much time do you take each day to sit at the Lord's feet? Ouch! For many of us, it seems easier to live life as Martha than as Mary. We have so much to do, so many projects to accomplish. It's hard to find time to spend with Jesus. But a life in balance will carve out time with the Lord.

Too Stressed Out to Seek God

If someone were to set to music Jesus' visits to the home of Mary and Martha, the second visit would begin in a minor key. In the first visit Luke focused on the two sisters, but as the apostle John reports the second visit he reveals that they had a brother, Lazarus. In John 11 we join Jesus and his disciples as a messenger arrives from Bethany with an urgent request from Mary and Martha.

Jesus was staying "beyond the Jordan River . . . near the place where John was first baptizing" (John 10:40). The messenger had traveled from Bethany toward Jericho, snaking his way through the Judean wilderness. He had then forded the Jordan River and traveled north to the spot where he heard that Jesus might be ministering.

After traveling all day the messenger found Jesus and delivered his heartfelt plea from the two sisters. "Lord, the one you love is very sick" (11:3). Lazarus was dying, and these faithful sisters needed a miracle from God's Messiah to save him. Unfortunately, Lazarus probably died shortly after the messenger left Bethany. It took about one day to travel from Bethany to the region north of Jericho, and at least one day to return from north of Jericho to Bethany. Before making the journey to Bethany, Jesus "stayed where he was for the next two days" (11:6)—making a total of at least four days from the time the messenger left Bethany until Jesus arrived there. And on his arrival he was told that Lazarus "had already been in his grave for four days" (11:17).

Imagine the grief of Mary and Martha. They had watched helplessly as their brother suddenly took ill. Once they realized how serious his illness was, they had sent for the one person who could heal him. They knew from reports where Jesus was ministering. As they had watched their brother's condition deteriorate throughout the day, they must have known that the messenger would not reach Jesus in time. And yet they must have hoped against hope that Jesus had somehow sensed their need and already started toward Bethany. Glancing from Lazarus—to the door—then back to Lazarus, they desperately prayed that Jesus would arrive in time to heal their brother. But the door never opened. Jesus didn't come. And Lazarus died before the day ended.

The mind-numbing suddenness of Lazarus's death and burial struck Mary and Martha with the force of a Roman catapult stone. They quickly prepared his body for burial and put it in the family tomb before sundown. The family probably laid Lazarus to rest just about the time the messenger reached Jesus with the news of his illness.

Late the next day the messenger returned with still more disturbing news. Yes, he had found Jesus and delivered the message. No, Jesus was not following just behind. Jesus had seemed remarkably calm on hearing the news. After announcing, "Lazarus's sickness will not end in death" (11:4), Jesus decided to stay where he was for a few more days. No, Jesus did not say when—or if—he would come to Bethany.

Two additional days passed in a blur of grief and bewilderment. Why hadn't Jesus come? How could he have been so wrong about Lazarus's physical condition? Why had he seemed so unconcerned? Would he come to pay his respects? How should they respond? Friends, relatives, and neighbors surrounded Mary and Martha to offer comfort in their time of grief, but these two sisters couldn't get their minds off Jesus—or their brother, Lazarus.

Then someone ran into the house and whispered to Mary and Martha that Jesus and his disciples had been seen walking up the road from the Judean wilderness toward town. Mary could not bring herself to leave the house, but Martha rushed out to see the Lord.

Perhaps Martha's decision to meet Jesus as he entered the village came from her desire to be the ever-gracious hostess. Or perhaps it sprang from a deeper spiritual understanding of who Jesus was. In any case Martha went to greet the one who, had he come just four days earlier, could have prevented Lazarus's death. Her greeting contained a mixture of faith and sadness. "Lord, if you had been here, my brother would not have died" (11:21).

Martha and Mary had probably played—and replayed—the "if only" game countless times over the past few days. *If only Jesus had been here when Lazarus became ill. If only Jesus had arrived in time to heal our brother. If only . . .* The words had become such a frequent refrain that both sisters greeted the Lord the same way. When Mary later went out to meet Jesus, the first words from her lips were, "Lord, if you had been here, my brother would not have died" (11:32).

Two sisters consumed with grief. Stressed out by circumstances beyond their control. Struggling with disappointment. But Martha kept her sense of balance. Several important differences between Mary and Martha highlight Martha's ability to maintain perspective in this particular instance:

- Mary stayed home while Martha went out to meet Jesus. (11:20)
- Mary focused only on what Jesus could have done in the past (11:32), while Martha added, "But even now I know that God will give you whatever you ask." (11:21-22)
- Mary was consumed with grief (11:33), while Martha gained strength from the certainty of a future resurrection and her trust in Jesus as "the Messiah, the Son of God." (11:24, 27)

The specific details of Jesus' encounter with Mary and Martha are significant. In this particular event, Martha is the sister with the greater sense of balance and perspective. Both believed Jesus could have healed Lazarus while he was still alive. But once Lazarus died, Mary could only grieve. Martha, however, found stability by seeking out Jesus and trusting in his ability to solve life's problems.

Martha revealed her faith through her three confessions to Jesus. First, she believed Jesus could alter events and circumstances—even death. Benjamin Franklin wrote, "Nothing can be said to be certain, except death and taxes." Death is the last great unalterable. As long as there is life, there is hope. But can hope extend into the grave? Martha's answer was yes! Although Lazarus had been dead four days, Martha affirmed, "Even now I know that God will give you whatever you ask" (11:22).

Second, Martha believed her separation from Lazarus was only temporary. Her brother would live again. The pain and heartache she now felt would someday vanish, and God would reunite her with her brother. She affirmed that he would rise again, "when everyone else rises, on resurrection day" (11:24).

Third, Martha believed Jesus was the promised Messiah, who was also God's Son. Bible teachers focus on Peter's great confession at Caesarea Philippi: "You are the Messiah, the Son of the living God" (Matthew 16:16). But few notice that this woman of deep faith from Bethany came to the same settled conviction: "I have always believed you are the Messiah, the Son of God, the one who has come into the world from God" (John 11:27).

Martha could believe in Jesus' ability to influence the future because she understood who Jesus was. He was not just a good man. He was not just a prophet. He was not just a teacher. He was not just a miracle worker. He was Israel's Messiah, and he was the eternal Son of God.

How big is your Jesus? Do you believe he can make a genuine change in life's struggles? Do you believe he will someday be able to wipe every tear from your eyes? Do you believe he is the eternal Son of God? It's so easy to forget these great truths in the middle of our struggles. But this knowledge provides balance—and the ability to endure.

Martha maintained balance in her time of grief by looking beyond the physical loss of her brother to God, who created life, who sustained life, and who would some-day restore life. In viewing life from God's eternal perspective Martha found peace—yet she still had much to learn.

Now Martha wanted Mary to discover the same sense of understanding. After making her great confession, Martha "called Mary aside from the mourners and told her, 'The Teacher is here and wants to see you'" (11:28). Mary went to the Lord and "fell down at his feet" (11:32).

In each of Jesus' three visits to Bethany we find Mary kneeling at his feet. In the first visit she knelt at his feet to learn. Here she kneels at his feet to mourn. In the next visit she will kneel at his feet to worship. Mary struggled to maintain balance as she grieved over the death of her brother. But she instinctively knew she would find her answers at the feet of Jesus.

The crowd waited in curious anticipation as Jesus and the sisters went to the grave. They understood the depth of his love as they watched him weep. They speculated what might have happened had the Master arrived before Lazarus died. And they gasped when they heard him give the command to roll the stone away from the mouth of the tomb.

Martha spoke and expressed the thought that must have been in everyone's mind. "Lord, by now the smell will be terrible because he has been dead for four days" (11:39). We know he's dead. Please let us remember him as he was when we put him in the tomb . . . wrapped in clean linen and covered with fragrant perfume. Don't remind us again of the awful corruption of death.

Jesus gently reminded Martha of the need to believe, to keep trusting in difficult times. Then he shouted, "Lazarus, come out!" (11:43). Had we been there as photographers for the *Jerusalem Post,* it would have been difficult to decide which scene was more dramatic. Turn your camera to the left and photograph a man wrapped like a mummy staggering to the entrance of the tomb. Or turn your camera to the right and photograph the faces of the crowd watching Lazarus come from the tomb. Eyes wide open, jaws hanging slack, bodies frozen in place—hands half-raised in fright and amazement.

Martha and Mary must have rushed over to release their brother from the graveclothes—the last vestiges of death still holding Lazarus in their grip. Mourning turned to feasting as the sisters welcomed their brother back from the grave. And they understood the importance of trusting God to maintain stability and balance in a chaotic world. God's eternal power is not reserved only for the sweet by-and-by; it's available to us in the stressful here and now.

Too Preoccupied to Worship God

Two visits to the home of Mary and Martha. Two very different occasions. Two women growing in their faith, each demonstrating great balance at different times. But we must stop by the hometown of these remarkable women one more time. It's early spring, and Passover is just six days away.

Tomorrow Jesus will ride a colt down the Mount of Olives into Jerusalem as thousands of cheering Jews cry, "Praise God! Bless the one who comes in the name of the Lord! Hail to the King of Israel!" (John 12:13). Five days later Jesus will be crucified. But tonight the mood is relaxed and festive. Jesus is attending a banquet given in his honor.

John does not tell us where in Bethany the banquet was held, but Matthew reports that it took place "at the home of Simon, a man who had leprosy" (Matthew 26:6). Perhaps the banquet was given by Simon or his family to honor the one who had healed him of his leprosy.

The banquet may have been held in Simon's home, but Mary, Martha, and Lazarus all attended. "Martha served, and Lazarus sat at the table with him" (John 12:2).

Somehow I expected to find Martha serving. All of us know individuals who live to serve—and we thank God for their unselfish generosity. We live in a society that selfishly demands all its rights and scoffs at "suckers" who put the needs of others ahead of their own. But the way of Christ runs counter to that of the world. Paul instructed the church at Philippi, "Don't be selfish; don't live to make a good impression on others. Be humble, thinking of others as better than yourself. Don't think only about your own affairs, but be interested in others, too, and what they are doing. Your attitude should be the same that Christ Jesus had" (Philippians 2:3-5).

If we desire to model our lives after Christ, we need an attitude of service. Martha had a servant's heart—and she is never condemned for that attitude. "But wait!" you say. "This chapter isn't on service; it's on balance." And you are right. Service, activity, kind deeds, assistance, help. All are important, but they can also become out of balance in an individual's life. How? Watch the events unfold in John 12.

The banquet in Bethany must have been a grand affair. In addition to Simon the leper, Jesus, and Lazarus, the guests included Jesus' disciples and a large crowd of Jews who came to see Jesus and Lazarus. In a typical banquet style adopted from the Greeks and Romans, the guests reclined around the outside of a low table shaped like the capital letter *E* with the middle bar removed. Each guest reclined on mats or pillows, with his feet angling away from the table. He leaned on his left elbow while eating with his right hand. Martha and the other servers would bring the food to the inside of the table to serve.

All the activity focused around the table facing toward the inside. I suspect no one even saw Mary slip around the outside of the table toward Jesus' feet. Perhaps it took a few seconds before one of the guests paused, sniffed the air, and looked around to see the source of the strong odor filling the room. There was Mary on her knees, pouring nearly a pint of pure nard on the feet of Jesus!

Nard, a fragrant oil, was normally applied in small quantities to the head. The apostle John carefully notes that Mary used "expensive perfume made from essence of nard" (12:3). How expensive? Judas, the treasurer (who, John notes, was also a thief and a traitor!), did a quick mental calculation. That amount of pure nard sold for about three hundred denarii, a year's wages for the average worker in Judea!

Judas feigned concern over Mary's extravagance. "It should have been sold and the money given to the poor" (12:5). However, John records Judas's real motive: "Not that he cared for the poor—he was a thief who was in charge of the disciples' funds, and he often took some for his own use" (12:6). Judas said all the right words—for all the wrong reasons!

But while John focuses on Judas and his motives, another Gospel writer, Matthew, takes a critical look at the other disciples. Evidently, they were swayed by Judas's reasoning. "The disciples were indignant when they saw this. 'What a waste of money,' they said" (Matthew 26:8). They were in the business of doing good deeds for the kingdom, and Mary's actions seemed like a big waste of money. The disciples were out of balance.

What's more important than serving God, doing good, and helping others? The disciples knew the importance of serving others and, with the exception of hypocritical Judas, they felt the perfume could have been better used for God's glory by being sold. I'm sure they were indignant as they protested. How could this woman be so thoughtless in her extravagance! They missed the point—but Jesus was about to set them straight.

All heads snapped back to Jesus when he spoke—and

their eyebrows arched upward when he directed his rebuke at *them!* "Leave her alone. She did it in preparation for my burial" (John 12:7). The Gospel of Mark adds a few additional details to Jesus' explanation. "She has done what she could and has anointed my body for burial ahead of time" (Mark 14:8).

Jesus had been announcing his coming death for some time. Numerous times he had explained to his disciples "that he had to go to Jerusalem, and he told them what would happen to him there. He would suffer at the hands of the leaders and the leading priests and the teachers of religious law. He would be killed, and he would be raised on the third day" (Matthew 16:21). But no one took Jesus' words seriously—except Mary.

Mary must have heard Jesus' pronouncements of his coming death, taken them to heart, understood he was dying to purchase her salvation—and decided to show her love in one final act of worship. Perhaps the jar of nard was her most valued possession. Very likely it was her most costly. She would show her understanding, her acceptance, and her deep devotion by anointing her Lord before the time of his death and burial. This was not the impetuous action of an emotional admirer or a frivolous demonstration of conspicuous wealth. It was, instead, a sincere act of worship by a follower who knew—and believed—the words of her Lord.

Mary understood the necessity of balancing service with worship, but the disciples did not. Jesus' explanation must have disturbed those who had heard, but did not understand, his repeated reminders of his coming death. "You will always have the poor among you, but I will not be here with you much longer" (John 12:8). Opportunities to do good, to help others, to meet needs would always exist. But opportunities to worship and serve Jesus while he was still in their midst were limited. The disciples focused so much on serving others that they missed out on the opportunity they had to worship and serve the Lord.

When Jesus was asked to summarize the entire Mosaic law, he could do it in two commandments: "You must love the Lord your God with all your heart, all your soul, and all your mind" and "Love your neighbor as yourself" (Matthew 22:37, 39). The entire Mosaic law hung on two commands—and those commands had to be kept in balance.

Some individuals claim to love God while responding to others with anger, petty jealousy, insensitivity, or indifference. They have all the right beliefs, meet at the appropriate times for worship, pray and read their Bibles diligently—but ignore and mistreat those around them. Someone has described those people as being so heavenly minded they are no earthly good.

Yet other Christians get so wrapped up in serving others that they forget to worship God. They get so involved in the needs of the here and now that they lose sight of the God of eternity who expects—and deserves—their love and devotion. And eventually their spiritual lives become barren and sterile. Much like the church of Ephesus described by the apostle John in the book of Revelation, you can get so busy with "your hard work and your patient endurance" that you wake up one day and realize "you don't love [the Lord] or each other as you did at first!" (Revelation 2:2, 4). Activity, even noble service for the Lord, can become a mistress that draws our hearts away from God. And if it does, our lives will fly out of balance.

Mary understood—and she put the Lord first. He was more important than her possessions, more important than her reputation, more important than her service to others. He deserved her worship and devotion—and she put him first.

Lessons from Bethany

We stand beside Mary and Martha, waving good-bye as Jesus and his disciples depart from Bethany for the climb over the Mount of Olives to Jerusalem. The scent of nard still lingers in the house long after Jesus is gone. The broken pieces of the alabaster jar sit on a shelf in the corner, delicate reminders of the last banquet in Bethany with Jesus.

As the two sisters reflect on the Master's visits to their village and their home, they discuss the lessons they have learned. And the word that comes to mind most often is *balance.* Jesus taught them several important secrets for living a balanced life in a very unbalanced world.

Martha smiles as she admits that her workaholic nature often caused her to become distracted and frustrated—until Jesus reminded her of her need to balance activity with time for God and his Word.

Mary's eyes glisten, and a single tear slides down her cheek as she remembers how upset she was when Lazarus died. She refused to leave the house and meet the Lord—until Jesus personally sent for her. He taught her to trust in him and to seek him out when the stresses of life became too great to bear.

The sisters hug as they think about the events of the previous night. The disciples were so preoccupied with doing good—watching the bottom line—harboring resources—that they forgot their first love. Martha served, but Mary worshiped. And in doing so she revealed how much she understood that God's plan for his Messiah led toward death.

At that moment a faint commotion can be heard in the distance. The crowd surging into Jerusalem chants something in unison. Both sisters strain to hear the words. "Hosanna! Blessed is he who comes in the name of the Lord!" (Mark 11:9, NIV). Thousands of pilgrims shouting their support for Jesus, Israel's Messiah. But Mary—and Martha—know Jesus is riding toward his death, not the earthly kingdom of David. His only crown will be a crown of thorns piercing his forehead.

These two sisters would maintain their balance in a week that would take others from messianic expectations to desertion and denial. But they would keep their balance because the Master had taught them well.

Questions to Ponder

Balance is our ability to keep from going to extremes. Several elements characterize an individual who maintains a balanced Christian life:

1. A balanced Christian life is a life that includes time spent with God and his Word. How much

time do you spend "at the feet of Jesus" each day, studying his Word? Are you, like Martha, too busy to spend time with him? Choose "the one thing worth being concerned about," and establish a set time each day when you can study God's Word and pray.

2. A balanced Christian life is a life that views problems and disappointments from God's eternal perspective. Make a list of your personal frustrations and struggles. Is God big enough to take care of these problems? Ask him to do so, and seek to understand his eternal perspective.

3. A balanced Christian life is a life that will not allow materialism to hinder the worship of God. How faithfully do you attend church? To what extent have you used your personal possessions to demonstrate your love for God?

4. Memorize Ecclesiastes 3:1, and ask God to help you discover the proper "time" and "season" in your life for all activities—so you can lead a balanced life.

There is a time for everything, a season for every activity under heaven. (Ecclesiastes 3:1)

9

SEXUAL PURITY

If It Feels Good,
Why Not Do It?

The Names Have Been Changed to Protect the Innocent

While growing up I loved watching the police shows on television that were based on true stories. One program would begin, "The story you are about to see is true. The names have been changed to protect the innocent." Well, the same is true of the story I'm about to share. The names—and a few details—have been changed to protect innocent individuals, churches, and groups. But the story is tragically true.

Frank grew up in a good, moral home. He was the typical "boy next door" every mother wants her daughter to date—clean-cut, friendly, outgoing, handsome, intelligent, churchgoing. After graduating in the top 10 percent of his high school class, Frank went to a state university. There he started dating Brenda, a vibrant Christian woman who had also enrolled at the university. They first met in a meeting organized by one of several Christian groups on the university campus.

Frank and Brenda seemed the ideal couple. Both were outspoken Christians who regularly attended church and who became highly involved in the Christian group on campus where they had first met. Both enjoyed backpacking and cycling. Both took their studies seriously and did well academically. No one was surprised when Frank and Brenda announced their engagement at the end of their junior year.

Their relationship was good—but not perfect. As their time together took on deeper intimacy, Frank became more preoccupied with their physical relationship. Brenda set boundaries, but Frank constantly tried to overstep them—and he sometimes succeeded. On several dates (usually in times of passionate kissing and petting) he had even suggested that they have sexual intercourse. Brenda always said no, and Frank never pressed the issue further. His advances made Brenda a little uncomfortable, but she attributed his behavior to the male hormones surging through his body.

Frank and Brenda completed college and got married the same summer. They both found jobs in another city, moved their meager possessions, found a church where they felt comfortable, and started their new life as husband and wife. Both became actively involved in their new church, and the people loved them. They seemed like the perfect role models for the youth—a good example of how God intended marriage to work. The "icing on the cake" came a few years later when their first child was born.

But all was not well in Frank's life. He harbored secrets he was too ashamed even to share with Brenda. Secrets that dated back to his first year at the university. The campus had over twenty thousand students and was located in a large city. The size of the campus and the city gave Frank an opportunity to explore "the other side of life" in anonymity. It began with Frank's driving across town to buy pornographic magazines at a bookstore. Frank took the magazines home and masturbated as he stared at the pictures of the naked women.

Frank's fascination with soft-core pornography produced an intense, but short-lived, pleasure. Eventually all the naked bodies looked the same. His level of sexual satisfaction dropped. Frank found an adult bookstore in the city that sold hard-core pornography. Now the pictures included men and women engaged in sexual acts. Again Frank felt the rush of intense sexual pleasure—and again it gradually faded with time.

Like a drug user being forced to take ever increasing doses of narcotics to achieve the same high, Frank found his appetite for more sexually explicit material growing. He started watching pornographic movies; then he slipped into topless bars that featured "adult entertainment." The need for more explicit images to reach the same level of physical satisfaction continued. Though he knew it was wrong, Frank even tried to pressure Brenda into engaging in premarital sex to satisfy his growing appetite. She refused, and her stand for what he knew in his heart was right flooded him with guilt.

He went home from those dates and threw himself on his bed in tears, vowing to the Lord that he would never look at another pornographic magazine or watch another pornographic film—but he always did. No one knew of his secret life, so he had no one to hold him accountable. He finally rationalized his obsession with pornography by convincing himself it was only a temporary tool to satisfy his sexual urges until he and Brenda got married. Then he wouldn't need to look at any more pornography.

During the first six months of their marriage, Frank avoided all pornographic material. His physical relationship with Brenda was as pleasing as he had always imagined it would be. It all seemed to be turning out OK—until Frank found himself home alone one evening watching a movie on television. Though the television station had edited the movie for content, the sexual overtones brought back the arousal Frank had first felt when he sat in a darkened theater, watching pornographic films. Frank found himself mentally replaying those earlier films that had burned themselves into his memory.

Within a week Frank made his way to an X-rated theater in a nearby town. He sat in the theater waiting to be sexually aroused—but he left disappointed. Having held a real woman in his arms, the pictures flashing on the screen no longer brought the same sense of satisfaction. The beast within him was again growing and demanding to be fed—but now it would take more than mere pictures or films to satisfy his addiction.

Some men have extramarital affairs to fulfill their unresolved sexual fantasies. Others seek out prostitutes. For some reason Frank took an even more vile and despicable route: rape. Perhaps it was because all the magazines and movies had presented women as nothing more than sex objects designed to fulfill a man's needs. Perhaps it was because he sought anonymity for his actions. Perhaps it was because even prostitutes would not perform the sex acts he had seared into his mind. For whatever reason, Frank began stalking innocent women.

The police knew they had a serial rapist on their hands. Same part of town each time, same basic method of entry, same perverted need to show pornographic movies to the victims before the rape. But no one suspected Frank—until the night he was caught.

One alert apartment dweller saw someone in the shadows and called the police. The police arrested Frank before he even realized they were closing in. "There must be some mistake!" he protested as they handcuffed him and took him to the station to be booked. Brenda, his colleagues at work, and his friends at church could not believe the charges. "The police must have the wrong man! Frank could never commit such evil acts!"

But the police had the right man. His fingerprints matched those taken from the apartments where the previous rapes had been committed. His semen matched the samples recovered from some of the rape victims. And his victims identified him as the rapist in a police lineup. Everything Frank had struggled so hard to hide in the dark recesses of his "other life" now made the front page of the local newspaper.

At the trial, Frank's family had to endure painfully graphic testimony of the wicked deeds he had done. The "other side" of Frank was dirty and ugly. As victim after victim took the stand to testify, the horror of his actions grew. Innocent lives marred and scarred to satisfy the basest needs of a man who worked so hard to present himself to others as an "ideal" Christian.

Today Frank sits in a jail cell in a maximum-security prison. His family is shattered; his church still struggles with feelings of hurt and anger. Much like a mud slide sweeping down a hillside, Frank's arrest, trial, and conviction swept away his facade of decency and exposed the sin that lurked just beneath the surface.

It Could Never Happen to Me

Your first response to Frank's tragic life might be, "It could never happen to me." And in one sense you are probably correct. Most individuals do not resort to rape. But be careful before you lower your guard. You *are* vulnerable to sexual temptation. And the consequences can be just as deadly to your physical, emotional, and spiritual health as they were to Frank's.

The apostle Paul wrote to the church in Corinth, which was struggling with serious moral, personal, and interpersonal problems. In the middle of his letter he taught the people of Corinth a history lesson that focused on the children of Israel in the wilderness. Paul reminded his readers that a number of sins (including sexual immorality) destroyed an entire generation of Israelites in the wilderness (1 Corinthians 10:6-11). He then applied this lesson to the church in Corinth. "If you think you are standing strong, be careful, for you, too, may fall into the same sin" (10:12).

But why devote an entire chapter to the danger of sexual

immorality and the need for sexual purity? Isn't lying or pride or greed just as evil in God's sight? It's true that all sin is evil. Every sin is an affront to God's holiness. And yet, we must focus on the importance of sexual purity for two reasons.

First, the Bible says there is a sense in which sexual sins are in a different class from most other sins. Paul explained this distinction to the church at Corinth—a city with a reputation for sexual excess. (One euphemism for a prostitute in Paul's day was a "Corinthian girl"!) Paul cut through the niceties and underscored the bottom line: "Run away from sexual sin! No other sin so clearly affects the body as this one does. For sexual immorality is a sin against your own body. Or don't you know that your body is the temple of the Holy Spirit, who lives in you and was given to you by God?" (6:18-19).

Sexual sins desecrate God's living temples on earth. When a Christian engages in sexual immorality, he or she takes God's sacred dwelling place and dishonors it. Several years ago a so-called artist made headlines when he displayed a crucifix of Jesus in a jar of urine. Sacrilege! About the same time a movie came out that portrayed Jesus committing adultery. Blasphemous! But the apostle Paul's point is that Christians are doing the same thing when they soil God's temple in the sheets of sexual immorality.

Second, we must focus on sexual purity because sexual temptation in our society is rampant—and growing exponentially. A generation ago, parents worried about "girlie" magazines flaunting bare breasts or movies that presented sexually suggestive scenes. Today those images flash on our television screens during prime time. Now society offers a sexual smorgasbord on the Internet, distributes condoms in the classroom, and ridicules the idea that schools should teach abstinence as an answer to teenage pregnancy and AIDS. Sexually transmitted diseases are increasing at an alarming rate among today's teenagers—and the only sure solution is sexual purity.

Christians can become desensitized to the danger by all the sexual images bombarding them every day. Much like the proverbial frog in the kettle, we don't realize the effect all the advertising and programming is having on us—until it's too late. The number of Christians falling into the trap of sexual immorality is too great to ignore any longer. And the results are catastrophic!

"Thus Saith the Lord . . ."

The Bible is an unblinking, unflinching witness to the far-ranging consequences felt by those who violate sexual purity. Regardless of one's age, occupation, position in society, or financial resources, those who disobey God's moral standards do so at their own risk. The list of ruined lives and shattered families is disturbing. Here are some of the more prominent individuals who saw their lives marred by sexual sin.

THE INDIVIDUAL(S)	THE SIN	THE RESULTS
Jacob's oldest son, Reuben (Genesis 35:22; 49:3-4)	Had sexual relations with his father's concubine	Forfeited his blessing as the firstborn son

David and Bathsheba (2 Samuel 11–12)	David committed adultery with Bathsheba and killed her husband to hide his sin	Child died, wives violated, sword never departed from his house after this event
Amnon and Tamar (2 Samuel 13)	Amnon raped his half sister Tamar	Amnon was killed by Tamar's brother Absalom
Solomon and his many wives (1 Kings 11:1-13)	Large harem turned his heart away from God	God raised up adversaries and divided the kingdom
Hosea's wife, Gomer (Hosea 1–3)	Committed aultery and abandoned her husband and children	Ended up on the slave block before being bought back by Hosea

King Solomon began his reign as king by asking God for wisdom to "know the difference between right and wrong" (1 Kings 3:9). God granted Solomon his request, and the Bible characterizes the early part of Solomon's reign as a time of wisdom, righteousness, and national prosperity. In fact, the Bible says, "God gave Solomon great wisdom and understanding, and knowledge too vast to be measured" (4:29).

Sometime during this period Solomon recorded many of his wise observations on life. These were later collected into the book of Proverbs. These proverbs give insight to naive and inexperienced youth about how life really works. Solomon, the wise instructor, offered his sage advice to young adults standing at the starting line of life, about to begin their race as adults. It's no accident that one key theme in Proverbs 1–9 is sexual purity. Solomon identified sexual purity as essential for living life successfully. Sit at Solomon's side and listen to his wise advice:

> The lips of an immoral woman are as sweet as honey, and her mouth is smoother than oil. But the result is as bitter as poison, sharp as a double-edged sword. Her feet go down to death; her steps lead straight to the grave. . . . Run from her! Don't go near the door of her house! If you do, you will lose your honor and hand over to merciless people everything you have achieved in life. Strangers will obtain your wealth, and someone else will enjoy the fruit of your labor. Afterward you will groan in anguish when disease consumes your body. (Proverbs 5:3-5, 8-11)

Such wise words! Too bad Solomon didn't follow his own warnings! As we saw in chapter 3, this man with all the wisdom decided to play fast and loose with his own advice. Perhaps he thought he was so wise he could play with matches and not get burned. I can imagine Solomon thinking, *The naive certainly need to watch out for sexual temptation, but I'm mature enough and intelligent enough to enjoy all the pleasures without falling into the traps.* Experience proved him wrong.

At the end of his life this world-weary wise man wrote another book—a journal of his quest to find satisfaction in life. Sex certainly played a part in his quest. "I said to myself, 'Come now, let's give pleasure a try. Let's look for the "good things" in life.' . . . I hired wonderful singers, both men and women, and had many beautiful concubines. I had everything a man could desire!" (Ecclesiastes 2:1, 8). But did seven hundred wives and three hundred concubines bring Solomon happiness? No! Solomon ended this chapter in his life's journal by sadly concluding, "As I looked at everything I had worked so hard to accomplish, it was all so meaningless. It was like chasing the wind. There was nothing really worthwhile anywhere" (Ecclesiastes 2:11).

Solomon was wise enough to know early in life how he needed to live to please God. And he was wise enough to know—at the end of his life—that his decision to disobey God had produced nothing but emptiness, heartache, and bitterness. In spite of all his wisdom, Solomon had violated God's standards of sexual purity and paid the price for his sin.

How to Stay Clean in a Pigsty

As I'm typing this chapter I'm listening to a recording of ocean surf pounding against a rocky coastline, accompanied by the music of Beethoven's *Moonlight Sonata*. A single piano—often just a single note—playing in a minor key. The music is slow, haunting at times, brooding. It matches my mood as I think of the many Christians I know who have wrecked their lives on the rocky shoals of sexual immorality. Lives once full of promise are now hollow, empty, filled with remorse and regret.

Is there any hope for believers today? Can we live pure lives in the sexual pigsty of our culture? Thankfully, the answer is yes. We *can* live lives of sexual purity. Let's focus on the life of one individual who serves as a model for all who want to remain sexually pure: Joseph.

We're All Victims

Society has elevated "victimhood" to unprecedented heights. We are not to blame for our actions because we are "victims" of our racial background, biological background, family background, economic background, social background, or educational background. If anyone ever had the opportunity to justify his actions by claiming to be such a victim, it was Joseph.

Joseph was born into a home that we would euphemistically call "blended" but that might better be described as dysfunctional. The quarrels, plots, deception, intrigue, and infighting among this extended family sound like a modern-day soap opera. Joseph's father, Jacob, had two wives and two concubines, each of whom bore him children. Jacob's father-in-law tricked Jacob into marrying his oldest daughter, Leah, though Jacob really loved her younger sister, Rachel. One week after marrying Leah, Jacob also married Rachel. Both sisters competed for the affection and attention of their husband.

Jacob was a weak, ineffective husband and father. His daughter was raped, but he kept quiet about it and refused to act (Genesis 34:5). Instead, he got upset with two of his sons when they acted to avenge this evil deed (34:6-7, 25-31). Also, Jacob's oldest son had sexual relations with one of his concubines (35:22), and though Jacob knew of it, he did not rebuke his son at that time. Joseph grew up with a father who did not model character or strength of conviction.

Joseph could also claim to be a victim of interpersonal conflict with his brothers. As the firstborn son of Jacob's favorite wife, Joseph received special attention from his father. When Jacob returned to the land of Canaan, he heard that his brother, Esau, was coming to meet him. Jacob had fled years before, after deceiving his father and "stealing" Esau's blessing, and Esau had vowed revenge.

Fearing an attack, Jacob divided his family—putting those most precious in the back. "Jacob now arranged his family into a column, with his two concubines and their children at the front, Leah and her children next, and Rachel and Joseph last" (33:2). How would you feel if you were one of the other children?

Jacob's special treatment of Joseph continued as the child grew. The breaking point for the other brothers came when Jacob gave Joseph "a beautiful robe" (37:3). This "coat of many colors" (as we remember it from our days in Sunday school!) signaled Jacob's favoritism toward Joseph. "His brothers hated Joseph because of their father's partiality. They couldn't say a kind word to him" (37:4).

Jacob's unwise actions caused his other sons to ostracize Joseph. The more Jacob showered Joseph with special praise, the more resentful Joseph's brothers became. Their hatred boiled over when Jacob sent Joseph to check on them. "When Joseph's brothers saw him coming, they recognized him in the distance and made plans to kill him" (37:18).

While the brothers did not follow through with their initial plan, they did sell Joseph as a slave to a band of traders, who dragged him off to Egypt. Joseph went from being the favorite son of his father to being a foreign slave in Egypt. His journey into slavery took him "to Potiphar, an officer of Pharaoh, the king of Egypt. Potiphar was captain of the palace guard" (37:36).

By today's standards Joseph had every right to be bitter and angry. His family background was a mess; his father's passivity and favoritism had brought disharmony and hatred. Now he had been rejected and abandoned by his brothers, sold as a slave, stripped of his dignity, and dragged to a foreign culture with new values and expectations. Joseph had every excuse needed to justify giving up on God and living a life of sin. Instead, he maintained a life of purity and devotion. Let's go behind the scenes to see how he did it.

Joseph Accepted God's Standards

From favored son to slave! In a matter of days Joseph went from his father's tent in Beersheba to a dry cistern near Dothan to slavery in the house of a government official in Egypt. But Joseph never lost his faith in God—and God never abandoned Joseph. The book of Genesis states clearly, "The Lord was with Joseph and blessed him greatly as he served in the home of his Egyptian master" (Genesis 39:2).

Joseph's exemplary attitude, and the success he seemed to have in every task he was given, didn't escape Potiphar's notice. "Potiphar soon put Joseph in charge of his entire household and entrusted him with all his business dealings" (39:4). In today's terms, Joseph was a winner! Life handed him a pile of lemons—and he opened a successful lemonade stand.

But Joseph's success was not based on the power of positive thinking. It came directly from the hand of God. Joseph put God first in his life, and God took care of the rest. Count how many times God gets the credit for Joseph's success:

- The Lord was with Joseph and blessed him greatly. (39:2)
- The Lord was with Joseph, giving him success in everything he did. (39:3)
- The Lord began to bless Potiphar for Joseph's sake. (39:5)

God blessed Joseph for his faithfulness, and Joseph's life took on a rags-to-riches quality that must have astounded those who knew him when he first arrived in Egypt as a seventeen-year-old slave. Joseph now ran the estate of one of Egypt's most powerful officials. He also developed physically. The awkward youth who had come to Egypt was now "a very handsome and well-built young man" (39:6).

Good looking, successful, self-assured, winsome. Joseph's qualities won him many admirers, including one who had no business looking! Potiphar's wife soon "began to desire him" (39:7). Subtlety was not her strong suit. She "invited him to sleep with her" (39:7). We do not know exactly what attracted her to Joseph. That the previous verse described Joseph as handsome and well-built certainly implies she had a strong physical attraction to him. Perhaps young, virile Joseph seemed doubly attractive next to her older, less attentive husband. For whatever reason, she made Joseph an offer she felt he couldn't refuse.

Stop and put yourself in Joseph's place. Your family background contains polygamy, incest, and rape. Not the sort of history that instills strong moral character and convictions. The God your father claimed to serve allowed you to be dragged away as a slave. Why should you listen to him? You've been working hard, and your effort is finally starting to pay off. And now a powerful woman is throwing herself at you sexually. She wants you! She needs you! Satisfy her and she could open up countless avenues for advancement.

I suspect all these thoughts flashed through Joseph's mind in the few seconds following this woman's brazen offer. Joseph blinked, swallowed hard, and then refused her offer. Turned her down. Stopped her advance cold! Joseph stayed sexually pure by rejecting an offer that had to be hard to resist. How did he do it?

The Bible offers two reasons Joseph refused to have sexual relations with Potiphar's wife. The first reason involved trust. Potiphar had entrusted Joseph with great responsibility. "My master trusts me with everything in his entire household. . . . He has held back nothing from me except you, because you are his wife" (39:8-9). Having sexual relations with this woman would violate a trust Potiphar had placed in Joseph. Joseph could not bring himself to break that trust.

But Joseph had a second reason for refusing this woman's offer, a reason even more compelling. "How could I ever do such a wicked thing? It would be a great sin against God" (39:9). God established standards for sexual purity and marital faithfulness at Creation. To commit adultery with another man's wife was a "wicked thing" and a violation of God's moral standards. As such, it was a "sin against God." Joseph looked at her offer through God's eyes and saw its perversity. By accepting God's standards for moral conduct, Joseph saw the offer as the sin it really was.

How would you have responded had you been in that house in Joseph's place? Let's update the scene to make it more realistic for today. You are single, and you are flying to another town for a job interview. On the airplane you talk to the person sitting next to you. You find this person to be charming and witty—to say nothing of being incredibly good looking! You smile and say good-bye as you walk up the jet ramp into the terminal.

Imagine your surprise later in the day when you meet this individual again in the lobby of the office building where you have your interview! And then you learn that this person is chief operating officer of the organization! Your meeting is highly successful, and when it's over the individual invites you to dinner. The meal is delightful, the conversation relaxed and friendly. You are having such a wonderful time. You are mildly surprised when you discover your host is not only warm and friendly, but also married, incredibly wealthy, and very lonely.

As the candles flicker softly, your host reaches across the table, caresses your hand, and says quietly, "I'm almost embarrassed to say this to you, but you are incredibly sexy and attractive. I find myself being drawn to you physically. I know this will sound forward, but I would very much like to spend the night with you."

You have nothing to lose. You enjoy this person's company. You know this night could open up great opportunities for personal advancement. None of your friends will ever know. As the sea of sexual fantasy churns around you, where can you drop your moral anchor to give yourself stability? Joseph teaches us that our moral anchor must rest on the bedrock of God's absolute standards of right and wrong. Sexual immorality is wrong, and those who commit immoral acts sin against God.

Joseph Avoided Tempting Situations

Question: How do you swallow an elephant?
Answer: One bite at a time.

Sometimes silly statements can contain a great deal of truth. On the positive side, you can often accomplish a project that seems too difficult by breaking it down into smaller pieces. As I started writing this book, the breadth of the subject discouraged me. But when I decided to tackle the project one bite—or one chapter—at a time, it eventually came together.

But this truth has a darker side. Christians who might never agree to plunge completely into a life of sin are often enticed into that sin "one bite at a time." Few individuals go directly from a life of sexual purity to gross sexual immorality. Small choices litter the pathway to sexual immorality—little compromises—incremental movements that take the individual ever closer toward the edge. The major temptations are easy to spot; the incremental compromises are often more subtle.

Joseph said no to Potiphar's wife, but she refused to take no for an answer. Her motto must have been, If at first you don't succeed, try, try again! She made the same offer to Joseph "day after day" (Genesis 39:10). I assume she tried slight variations on the same basic theme. Perhaps one day she wore her most revealing dress. The next day she spent extra time putting on her makeup. The next day she used the most fragrant perfumes. The next day she tried a subtle touch as she whispered in his ear. The approach varied, but the offer never changed: Come to bed with me! Potiphar's wife intended to get Joseph—even if she had to draw him in "one bite at a time."

Joseph had a problem! Sexual temptation was ever present, ever compelling, ever available. As a slave Joseph had no control over his place of residence. But he could, to some extent, avoid tempting situations. He adopted a twofold strategy to fight off this woman's advances: (1) Refuse all direct offers to commit sexual immorality and (2) avoid all tempting situations. Joseph "refused to sleep with her, and he kept out of her way as much as possible" (39:10).

Were the danger of sexual sin not so serious, we could almost find Joseph's actions comical. Joseph rearranged his entire schedule to avoid being in a room alone with

Potiphar's wife. If she was supervising the kitchen staff, Joseph was checking on the livestock. If she went out into the garden, he managed to find a reason to go inside to inventory the storehouse. Joseph was a wise man!

In a society saturated with sexual images and offers, it's easy for us to get sucked into sin "one bite at a time." Some who struggle with pornography still stop to look at the magazine racks in stores. They scan the shelves, their eyes looking for magazines that bring cheap thrills but no lasting satisfaction. Others watch the daytime soap operas, confusing true romance with the tawdry affairs and shallow physical relationships that spew from the television every afternoon.

So what's the danger in watching a soap opera, looking at photographs of naked women, seeing one graphic sex scene in a popular film, or reading a graphic sex scene in a novel? It's not as if we are having an affair ourselves, is it? Yes, it is! Sexual immorality begins in the mind, in agreeing to tolerate, then enjoy, then long for, then seek out experiences God reserves for marriage.

Jesus understood the fact that sexual purity (and sexual immorality) begins in the mind and heart when he said, "You have heard that the law of Moses says, 'Do not commit adultery.' But I say, anyone who even looks at a woman with lust in his eye has already committed adultery with her in his heart" (Matthew 5:27-28). The attitude precedes the act. Sometimes the best defense against sexual temptation is to physically avoid those situations where we can be tempted.

Jesus makes this point by using hyperbole to explain

how to avoid sexual temptation. "If your eye—even if it is your good eye—causes you to lust, gouge it out and throw it away" (5:29). He is *not* teaching self-mutilation. Rather, he is saying, Don't think you can keep looking at a woman and lusting after her without sinning! You would be better off blind—so you couldn't look at her and lust!

A better solution is not to put yourself in a place where you have the opportunity to look at the woman and lust. To keep his mind pure, Joseph avoided those situations where he could be tempted. Avoidance is a good technique for sexual purity. Only you and God know the specific areas where you struggle sexually. Admit your weakness and vow to avoid ever putting yourself in a place where you can be tempted in that area. It might change where you shop, what you watch on TV, or where you go on vacation, but it's a small price to pay for sexual purity.

Joseph Refused to Give In to Sin

Joseph's plan to avoid tempting situations was fundamentally sound. Under normal circumstances, taking such precautions would do much to keep an individual pure. But Potiphar's wife was anything but normal! Joseph made an elusive target, but Potiphar's wife remained persistent—and cunning.

This wily woman carefully constructed her trap for Joseph. She first removed the other household servants. I imagine she sent some to the market, others into the fields, still others on insignificant but time-consuming errands. Joseph would be unable to run to a servant and use that individual to escape. No, this time it would just be she and

Joseph in the house alone, and she would have him to herself.

"No one else was around when he was doing his work inside the house" (Genesis 39:11). The sound from Joseph's sandled feet bounced off the empty halls and echoed back into his ears. The house was quiet—too quiet. At first, Joseph had focused so intently on his duties that he hadn't noticed the silence. Now the eerie quiet made him stop and listen. Not a sound.

Joseph put aside his work and softly began to walk through the house. Where were the servants? Why was the work not being done? Who had changed the schedule Joseph had posted for the day? Joseph was so preoccupied that he didn't notice the lone shadow darting across the open doorway in front of him.

Joseph jumped as delicate—but powerful—hands grabbed the shoulders of his linen cloak and pulled. As the garment started to slip from his body, a sensuous, demanding voice spoke from the shadows: "Sleep with me!" (39:12).

Turning, Joseph saw Potiphar's wife. Her seductive dress and leering eyes left no doubt as to her intentions. She wanted sex with Joseph. Now! On her terms! In her bed! Joseph was trapped. Alone in the house. Facing a woman mad with passion.

Some might say, Why bother to fight it? This powerful woman will eventually get what she wants. Joseph is just a slave in her home—with no more rights than a piece of property. If she wants sex, what can Joseph do to stop her advances? Laws governing sexual harassment did not exist.

Joseph's solution was swift, dramatic, and effective! "Joseph tore himself away, but as he did, his shirt came off. She was left holding it as he ran from the house" (39:12). Run! Flee! Vamoose! Head for the hills! Joseph got his feet in gear and set an Egyptian record for the hundred-yard dash. And in doing so he became the world's first "streaker"—running away without even stopping to wrestle his clothes from the hand of the woman who had ripped them off his body.

When unexpected sexual temptations catch you off guard, don't take time to analyze, theorize, rationalize, or compromise. Get out! Immediately! The apostle Paul may have had Joseph in mind when he wrote about sexual temptations. The way to maintain sexual purity is to *flee*—just as Joseph did. Paul didn't mince words. His advice to those believers living in the moral cesspool called Corinth was, "Run away from sexual sin!" (1 Corinthians 6:18). Just over a decade later he gave the same advice to his young disciple, Timothy. "Run from anything that stimulates youthful lust" (2 Timothy 2:22).

What's the secret to sexual purity? Start by making God's standards your own. "Don't you know that those who do wrong will have no share in the Kingdom of God? Don't fool yourselves. Those who indulge in sexual sin . . . adulterers, male prostitutes, homosexuals . . . none of these will have a share in the Kingdom of God" (1 Corinthians 6:9-10). God condemns all forms of sexual immorality. Agree with God that sexual purity is the only acceptable standard, and make it your standard.

If you have made a commitment to remain sexually

pure, what can you do to keep your vow? First, follow Joseph's example and avoid tempting situations. Watch your choice of television programs, movies, and magazines. Don't allow yourself to get into a situation where you will be tempted. Second, if you ever find yourself in a situation where you are being tempted, flee! Get up, walk out, and put as much distance between you and the temptation as possible. Don't allow the temptation to gain a foothold in your mind.

What If I've Failed?

I'm enough of a realist to know that my words have reached some of you too late to keep you from sexual impurity. Some of you struggle with an addiction to pornography. Others carry a burden of guilt from past sexual immorality, including premarital sex or adulterous affairs after marriage. What can you do if you have already crossed God's barrier and entered the forbidden zone of sexual immorality?

First, realize that God can, and does, forgive all sin, including the sin of sexual immorality. Our responsibility is to confess our sin—to acknowledge to God that we were wrong and he is right. "If we confess our sins to him, he is faithful and just to forgive us and to cleanse us from every wrong" (1 John 1:9). Why not stop reading right now and confess your sins to your heavenly Father? If you confess, he will forgive.

Second, commit in your heart to remain sexually pure for the rest of your life. You cannot undo your past—but you can choose your direction for the future. Follow the example of Joseph by committing to remain pure, avoiding tempting situations, and fleeing direct temptations.

Third, bathe your mind in God's Word. One sad reality of sexual immorality is that the sexual images are burned into our minds. Pornographic magazines, explicit movies, and extramarital sexual encounters leave lasting memories—and these memories can be as powerful a temptation to you as Potiphar's wife was to Joseph.

God provides a solution to the "mind pollution" you may have already suffered: the cleansing power of his Word. "Don't copy the behavior and customs of this world, but let God transform you into a new person by changing the way you think" (Romans 12:2).

Filling your mind with God's Word, hiding it in your heart, is God's method for cleansing your mind of the toxic waste left by past immorality. Psalm 119 focuses on the benefits of God's Word, especially for gaining mastery over temptation and sin. "How can a young person stay pure? By obeying your word and following its rules" (119:9). "Your word is a lamp for my feet and a light for my path" (119:105). "Guide my steps by your word, so I will not be overcome by any evil" (119:133). Haunted by memories of past immorality? Start cleansing your mind by filling it with the Word of God.

Fourth, remember that sin has consequences. God can forgive your past sin—but forgiveness doesn't always eliminate sin's consequences. If you have sexual relations with someone to whom you are not married, it is sin. God can forgive the sin. However, if you contract AIDS, syphilis, or any of a host of other sexually transmitted diseases, God will not automatically take it away when you confess. You can receive God's forgiveness for committing rape, but God also ordained human government—and it will imprison you for your crime.

Sexual sin is serious, and the consequences can linger long after you confess and receive forgiveness. If you have sinned and have confessed to God, realize that one consequence of your sin may be a limit on your future service for him. Be content to serve God in whatever capacity he graciously allows. Also, realize you will need to earn the trust of those you hurt most by your past failure. Make yourself accountable, and prove yourself trustworthy. Earning back trust is a slow process—but the results are worth the effort.

Questions to Ponder

Sexual purity stands as one of the great defining characteristics of a faithful child of God. Yet many Christians struggle to remain sexually pure.

1. An axiom for today's computer age is "Garbage in, garbage out." What you feed into your mind eventually shows up in how you live. Do you struggle with pornography? What types of magazines and movies are you reading and watching? Would you be embarrassed to have Jesus sit beside you while you read, watch TV, or attend a movie? Avoid any magazines, television programs, and movies that can't pass the Jesus test.

2. Are you now experiencing any sexual temptations?

What specifically can you do to avoid these situations? Seek out an individual you can trust and ask him or her to hold you accountable in this area.

3. Are you guilty of past sexual immorality? If so, have you confessed your sin to God? Why not make a specific commitment, right now, to live the rest of your life in sexual purity?

4. Memorize 1 Corinthians 6:18, and ask God to give you the ability to flee all sexual immorality from now on.

Our bodies were not made for sexual immorality. They were made for the Lord, and the Lord cares about our bodies. (1 Corinthians 6:13)

10

ENDURANCE

*How Do I Develop
Spiritual Stamina?*

Rudy

In 1974 Daniel "Rudy" Ruettiger transferred into Notre
Dame University and tried out as a walk-on player for the
Notre Dame football team. Since childhood, Rudy had
dreamed of playing football for Notre Dame. Now he
wanted to prove to everyone that he was a doer, not just a
dreamer.

Neither the coaches nor the players believed Rudy could
succeed. He was just too small, too slow, too *average* to
have any chance of making the team. But Rudy proved
them all wrong. His grit, determination, and heart more
than made up for his size and limited athletic ability. Rudy
made the scout team—the group of unknowns with the
thankless job of helping the main squad prepare for each
week's game. Glorified tackling dummies!

Rudy threw himself into the role. Though he only had
a fraction of the athletic ability of the starting players, he
exerted twice the effort. His persistence and desire inspired
other members of the team. For two years he served on the

scout team. Bruised, beaten up, battered—but never broken in spirit. Rudy lived out his dream.

In the final game of his senior year the starting players persuaded the coach to allow Rudy to "suit up" for the game. In the closing seconds the coach sent him in from the sidelines, and Rudy made one spectacular play. As the game ended, the other players hoisted Rudy onto their shoulders and carried him off the field. Rudy was a winner!

Rudy Ruettiger's inspiring story touches a tender spot in all our hearts. We *like* stories that focus on individuals who endure in spite of adversity—who persevere to overcome great obstacles. The true story of Rudy made a wonderful motion picture.

What's Wrong with This Picture?

We love stories of individuals who overcome and persevere—but our perception is often distorted. We focus on the happy ending and forget the pain and struggle it took to get there. We imagine ourselves being hoisted onto the shoulders of the other Notre Dame players and forget the two years of physical punishment and pounding Rudy Ruettiger endured to earn the right to sit on those shoulders.

A little bit of Walter Mitty lives in us all. Walter Mitty is James Thurber's fictional character who spent most of his dreary life daydreaming about great exploits—starring himself as the hero, of course! Walter Mitty dreamed great dreams, but he never bridged the chasm between dreaming and doing. The world has a surplus of Walter Mittys—and a shortage of Rudy Ruettigers.

What separates the dreamers from the doers? One big difference is endurance. All of us dream, but few are willing to pay the price required to make those dreams reality. When the going gets tough, most stop going! Endurance is the ability to stay the course—to pay the price—to keep going when everyone else says it's time to quit.

When the Going Gets Tough

The prophet Jeremiah served God at a time when God's prophets were not popular. The people of Judah refused to respond to Jeremiah's call to repentance. One time Jeremiah thought the people were about to respond. But God opened his eyes to the harsh reality of human sinfulness. "I had been as unaware as a lamb on the way to its slaughter. I had no idea that they were planning to kill me!" (Jeremiah 11:19).

Innocent, unsuspecting Jeremiah suddenly saw behind the smiling faces and understood what the people actually thought of him, his message, and his God. Jeremiah cried out in discouragement, and God reminded him of the need for endurance. "If racing against mere men makes you tired, how will you race against horses? If you stumble and fall on open ground, what will you do in the thickets near the Jordan?" (12:5).

Sometimes it helps our own understanding of the Bible if we translate God's thoughts into the language of today. God threw a cold bucket of reality on Jeremiah and said, Jeremiah, if you are struggling to make it through the Boston Marathon, what will you do when I enter you in the Kentucky Derby? If you stumble on rock-covered roads, what will you do when I hand you a machete and have you hack your way through impenetrable jungle? Prepare yourself, Jeremiah. It will get harder before it gets easier!

So how would you feel if you were Jeremiah? (Anyone who says "Great!" needs to go back and read the chapter on honesty!) None of us likes pain, struggle, or hardship. But sometimes that is the only way God can accomplish the work that must be done in our lives.

It Is Well

Hanging in the lobby of Jerusalem's American Colony Hotel is a handwritten poem. Neither the penmanship nor the paper gives this poem its special place on the wall. Its author, Horatio Spafford, scratched out the words on a sheet of hotel stationery. The poem is special because of the grandeur of its thoughts—and the circumstances that led to its writing.

Philip Bliss later set the words to music, and the hymn "It Is Well with My Soul" remains a classic Christian song of hope. Of all the Christian songs I know, this simple song by Spafford and Bliss touches my soul like no other. What prompted Spafford to write the words of the song— and how those words ended up on the lobby wall of this venerable Jerusalem hotel—is, as Paul Harvey would say, *the rest of the story.*

Horatio Spafford lived in Chicago in the late 1800s. Friends would describe Spafford as a family man, a law-yer—and a Christian. Yet within the space of two short years this Christian gentleman saw his world collapse. In

October 1871 the Great Chicago Fire wiped out Chicago's central business district—including Spafford's law offices. The fire also decimated Chicago's economy, threatening several real-estate ventures in which Spafford had invested heavily. One year later these ventures failed. Both the fire and the real-estate failure hurt Horatio Spafford financially. But the worst was yet to come.

Spafford sent his wife and four children on a trip to Europe while he tried to put his personal finances back in order. His family set sail on the *Ville du Havre,* one of the premier passenger ships sailing the Atlantic Ocean. But on November 21, 1873, the *Ville du Havre* was struck by another vessel and sank in the cold waters of the North Atlantic. Spafford's wife miraculously survived the shipwreck—but all four children were lost at sea. The cable Spafford received from his wife described the magnitude of their loss in two simple words: *SAVED ALONE.*

As soon as he received the cable, Spafford boarded a train for the East Coast to book passage on the next available ship. He wanted—he needed—to be with his wife in this time of sorrow and tragedy. During the journey across the Atlantic the captain summoned Spafford to his cabin as the ship reached the spot where the *Ville du Havre* had gone down.

Stop and put yourself in Horatio Spafford's place. Grief stricken. Alone. Financially drained. Physically drained. Emotionally drained. How would you fare under the hammer blows of trouble he had faced? When all life's crutches and supports are kicked away, how well will you be able to stand?

Horatio Spafford left us two written records that serve as windows into his soul during this dark, lonely period. The first is a letter he wrote to a sister-in-law:

> On Thursday last we passed over the spot where she went down, in mid-ocean, the water three miles deep. But I do not think of our dear ones there. They are safe, folded, the dear lambs, and there, before very long, shall we be too. In the meantime, thanks to God, we have an opportunity to serve and praise him for his love and mercy to us and ours. "I will praise him while I have my being." May we each one arise, leave all, and follow him.[1]

Pause for just a second and read those words again, slowly. How could Horatio Spafford speak of "love," "mercy," and "praise" in such a time of sorrow? What gave him the ability to thank God in the midst of such personal pain? How could he endure—and turn tragedy into triumph?

Spafford shared his secret in his other writing, his poem that now hangs in the hotel lobby. In this poem Spafford opened his heart as he put his thoughts to verse. Imagine for a moment that you are Horatio Spafford, and read these words as if you had just written them on a piece of hotel stationery with your fountain pen.

> *When peace like a river attendeth my way,*
> *When sorrows like sea-billows roll;*
> *Whatever my lot, Thou has taught me to know,*
> *"It is well, it is well with my soul."*

Though Satan should buffet, though trials should come,
Let this blest assurance control,
That Christ hath regarded my helpless estate,
And hath shed his own blood for my soul.

My sin—O the bliss of this glorious thought,
My sin, not in part but the whole,
Is nailed to his cross and I bear it no more,
Praise the Lord, praise the Lord, O my soul!

And, Lord, haste the day when the faith shall be sight,
The clouds be rolled back as a scroll,
The trump shall resound, and the Lord shall descend,
A song in the night, oh my soul![2]

How could Spafford respond with such assurance, joy, and peace? His was not a natural response. God had *taught* him to say "It is well with my soul." He endured because he grasped God's purpose, God's protection, and God's plan in the events that seemed to swirl out of control all around him. Horatio Spafford and his wife continued to live their lives for God. Eventually they traveled to Jerusalem to help start the American Colony, a group dedicated to sharing Christ's love with the Muslim and Jewish inhabitants of that sacred city. Spafford died, and was buried, in Jerusalem. The building used by these early missionaries eventually became the American Colony Hotel—and the poem penned by Spafford still hangs on its walls. *And now you know the rest of the story!*

Well Done, Thou Good and Faithful Servant

The last time I heard Spafford's haunting words my eyes misted over and a lump formed in the back of my throat. I had just delivered a eulogy for a dear friend who had died in an automobile accident, and the soloist who followed me sang "It Is Well with My Soul." I sat on the platform looking out into the audience, but my eyes kept drifting back to the closed coffin just below me. I stared at the wooden box that held the earthly remains of a remarkable man. It seemed as if much of Odessa, Texas, agreed with me because the church was full of friends who had come to say good-bye.

What was it about this man that allowed him to make such an impact on others? From my own experience I felt confident that it was his character and integrity. He was quiet, unassuming, humble, compassionate, caring, thorough, committed to excellence. When I read through some of the cards and letters before the service, I saw phrases like "an inspiration to teachers," "a model for others," "an influence to me," and "an encourager."

This dear saint and his wonderful wife made an impact on others because they consistently lived for Jesus Christ. In good times and bad. In easy times and hard. In times of joy and sorrow. In times of ease and struggle. They endured—and triumphed! Two days before the accident that ultimately took his life, this quiet man shared with a friend his confidence that we live each day preparing ourselves for eternity—and he was prepared. Much like Enoch in the Old Testament, he "enjoyed a close relationship with God throughout his life. Then suddenly, he disappeared because God took him" (Genesis 5:24).

My friend's life can be summarized in three words. He *endured, persevered,* and *triumphed.* From a human perspective his life ended suddenly, abruptly. But God doesn't make mistakes. This man of God lived every moment of his life as if it might be his last, and he was ready when God called him to heaven. As I sat on the platform of the church, I wiped a tear from my cheek and thought about the first words he may have heard when he opened his eyes in heaven. Perhaps words like, "Well done, thou good and faithful servant . . . enter thou into the joy of thy lord" (Matthew 25:21, KJV).

Let's Make a Deal

The houselights dim, a single spotlight focuses on the center of the stage, and the ever smiling host leaps from between the curtains. You are the first contestant today on the game of life. The host extends his arm to the left, and a curtain opens. Behind the curtain are pictures of the Magic Kingdom, Epcot, and the Disney-MGM Studio. "The first option available to our contestant today is an all-expense-paid trip to Orlando, Florida. Select this prize, and you can enjoy the time of your life in Disney World!"

The host then turns to his right and extends his arm to another curtain. As his hand points to the curtain, it opens, revealing a coffin! The announcer continues. "The second option available to our contestant today is an all-expense-paid trip to a funeral. Select this option, and you can spend a day with those mourning over the death of a loved one."

What? Who in their right mind would *ever* choose option number 2? Given a choice, we *all* would select pleasure over pain, happiness instead of heartache. And then our heads snap around as a voice from the back of the room says softly, "Sorrow is better than laughter, for sadness has a refining influence on us. A wise person thinks much about death, while the fool thinks only about having a good time now" (Ecclesiastes 7:3-4). We stare into the time-worn face of wise old Solomon and ponder the meaning of his words.

Some have misunderstood Solomon's words. He did *not* oppose pleasure. Throughout the book of Ecclesiastes Solomon urged his readers to enjoy the life God had given them. "That is indeed a gift from God" (5:19). Solomon's point in Ecclesiastes 7 was not to condemn pleasure. Rather, it was to remind us that we gain wisdom in times of pain, not in times of pleasure.

Our family lives about forty-five minutes from Six Flags over Texas, a large amusement park in the Dallas/Fort Worth metroplex. When our children were younger we usually went to Six Flags at least once each summer. Ride the carousel. Buy something to drink. Ride the gas-powered cars. Buy something to eat. Ride the small roller coaster. Buy something to drink again. The day raced by as we ran from one ride to another. Sometime after dark we would walk, zombie-like, out to the car and drive home, exhausted but happy.

I enjoyed visiting Six Flags. It was fun! But I have a confession. At no time during any of my visits did I ever think deep theological thoughts, make any profound decisions, or come to any startling conclusions about life. Happy times are usually not the times when we think deeply about life.

The times we stop to reflect on the ultimate realities of life are usually moments of deep sorrow and mourning. Funerals are occasions when normally busy people stop and ask the more profound questions of life. What is life's ultimate purpose? What happens after death? What really is important in this life? Solomon understood a profound paradox of life. Though I naturally prefer times of pleasure to times of pain, those times of pain are necessary for my personal development.

The Testing of Your Faith

James, the half brother of our Lord Jesus Christ, understood Solomon's profound words. Writing to those facing pain and suffering, James opened his book with words as startling as those penned by Solomon almost ten centuries earlier. "Dear brothers and sisters, whenever trouble comes your way, let it be an opportunity for joy. For when your faith is tested, your endurance has a chance to grow. So let it grow, for when your endurance is fully developed, you will be strong in character and ready for anything" (James 1:2-4).

The testing of faith produces endurance, and endurance produces strength of character and maturity. James reminded his readers that the proper response to problems will develop spiritual maturity. Endurance is a process that produces depth of character. But words alone can ring hollow. When individuals face life-and-death situations, they often need concrete images to help them stay focused.

James understood his audience's need to see God's truth put into shoe leather. Later in his book James pointed his readers to flesh-and-blood examples of patience and endurance. "For examples of patience in suffering, look at the prophets who spoke in the name of the Lord. We give great honor to those who endure under suffering. Job is an example of a man who endured patiently. From his experience we see how the Lord's plan finally ended in good, for he is full of tenderness and mercy" (5:10-11).

I grew up hearing about the "patience of Job" and reading about his "patience" in the King James Version of my Bible. Then I studied Greek and learned that James actually spoke of the *endurance* of Job. James used two different words to describe patience and endurance. The "prophets who spoke in the name of the Lord" displayed patience; Job demonstrated endurance. Let's face it: Job didn't always exhibit great patience! But he does stand as a model of endurance. Let's wander down to the ash heap to spend some time with Job and his friends.

The Endurance of Job!

Job lived most of his life in power and luxury. He served as the model for *Time* magazine's "Man of the Year" before *Time* magazine ever existed. In a day when society measured wealth in livestock, Job dominated the "stock market." He owned seven thousand sheep (he covered the clothing market!), three thousand camels (he corralled the transportation industry!), and five hundred teams of oxen and five hundred donkeys (he cornered the farming sector!). Simply put, "He was, in fact, the richest person in that entire area" (Job 1:3).

But while others clawed their way to the top by cutting corners or climbing over the backs of others, Job managed to reach the pinnacle of success with his integrity intact. "He was blameless, a man of complete integrity. He feared God and stayed away from evil" (1:1). Honest businessman. Faithful husband. Good father. Job was almost too good to be true.

Then, on one tragic day, the wheels came off. We learn in the first two chapters of the book that Job was a test case in the cosmic struggle between God and Satan. Satan challenged Job's motives and God's own worthiness to receive worship. "Satan replied to the Lord, 'Yes, Job fears God, but not without good reason! You have always protected him and his home and his property from harm. You have made him prosperous in everything he does. Look how rich he is! But take away everything he has, and he will surely curse you to your face!'" (1:9-11). Satan received God's permission to test Job, and Job never knew what hit him!

In the space of a few hours Job went from prince to pauper. Before one messenger could finish telling Job about a disaster, another messenger arrived with still more bad news. Foreign invaders stole all the oxen and donkeys. "The fire of God"—perhaps a freak thunderstorm—killed all the sheep. Foreign invaders stole all the camels. A freak windstorm blew over a house and killed all his children.

Bam! Four hammer blows of sorrow landed directly on Job.

But Satan was not through with Job. Having stripped Job of his wealth, Satan set out to rob him of his health. Satan "struck Job with a terrible case of boils from head to foot" (2:7). In misery and sorrow, Job "sat among the ashes" (2:8). Then Satan used Job's own wife to whisper the final words of temptation when Job was most vulnerable. "Are you still trying to maintain your integrity? Curse God and die" (2:9).

Though spoken out of hurt, anger, and sorrow for her stricken husband, the words of Job's wife still posed a haunting question. How could Job possibly maintain his integrity after being abandoned by God? After all, in two of the first four calamities God had not stepped in to protect Job from the attacks of others. And the other two calamities were things we even now refer to as "acts of God," pointing to God himself as the author of the evil now holding Job in its viselike grip.

How did Job survive spiritually when the wheels came off? What gave him his stability and his ability to endure in such trying circumstances? Job provided four answers in his extended debate with those who came to comfort him.

Endurance Comes from Looking Inward

Job remained on course spiritually because he set his internal compass properly. When Job lost everything, he reminded himself that the sovereign God who had granted him wealth also had the right to take it away. "Praise the name of the Lord!" (Job 1:21).

Job had no idea why he was suffering. He knew nothing of the contest between God and Satan. From Job's perspective, it seemed to be a case of mistaken identity. God had chosen to punish Job though Job was innocent. Job longed for an opportunity to meet with God face-to-face so he could clear his name. But from Job's perspective, even if God wrongly punished him, Job refused to stop living in a way that pleased God. "I make this vow by the living God, who has taken away my rights, by the Almighty who has embittered my soul. As long as I live, while I have breath from God, my lips will speak no evil, and my tongue will speak no lies" (27:2-4).

Others can take your reputation, your riches, your health, and even your happiness. But no one can take away your integrity, except you. Job's world fell apart. Right seemed to become wrong. Up became down. Righteousness brought pain instead of blessing. When life strips away all the external rewards and controls, what is your response? When you no longer must act a part or play a role expected by others, what will the "real" you say and do?

When Job reached the irreducible minimum, all he had left inside were his convictions and his integrity. Right *was* right; wrong *was* wrong. And Job refused to compromise on his convictions or his integrity. Job's final speech to his friends ended with his taking a series of oaths proclaiming his commitment to integrity. He began by attesting, "I made a covenant with my eyes not to look with lust upon a young woman" (31:1). In the following verses Job affirmed his commitment to sexual purity, honesty, justice, compassion, and faithfulness. In each case he stated on oath to God, If I have secretly sinned in this area, may I be judged for my actions!

Have you made a commitment similar to the one made by Job? Have you committed in your heart that, come what may, you will not depart from living a life of integrity? Whatever the temptation? Whatever the circumstances? Whatever the cost to you, personally or professionally? Looking inside and setting our internal moral compass is the first step in developing endurance.

Endurance Comes from Looking Upward

In the Boy Scouts we learned how to find our way through the woods using only a compass and a map. I always loved maps, and I had a good sense of direction. Each year at camp the different Boy Scout troops competed against one another to see which troop had best mastered the skills of knot tying, plant identification, swimming, and using a compass.

I remember the summer I represented our troop on the map course. Each Boy Scout received a written set of directions that read something like: "Walk on a 135-degree bearing for 65 feet, then turn and head on a bearing of 85 degrees for 40 feet, then . . ." Oh, did I mention that each participant had to wear a bag over his head while following these directions? The only things visible to each scout were his compass and his feet!

The judges spun the participants around to disorient them. The scouts then had to get their bearings and begin walking in the appropriate direction.

Picture a large, open field with ten Boy Scouts staggering around wearing paper bags over their heads. Nine seem to be going in the same general direction, but one appears to be moving away from the group at a 90-degree angle. With each step the gap between that one and the other nine grows larger. Now, imagine the look on that scout's face when he reaches what he thinks is the proper destination and pulls the bag off his head. Boy, did I feel stupid!

I'm not sure whether I misread the directions or misread my compass. But while all the other Scouts were zigging, I had been zagging, completely unaware of my error or of the snickers and guffaws of the spectators!

What went wrong? I learned that even using a compass, it's still easy to become disoriented. The bag over my head prohibited me from using fixed points in the surrounding area to help me find my way. On hikes in the mountains we used the compass to find our general direction. We then looked for fixed points (mountains, tall trees, the North Star, etc.) to help us keep our bearings. The compass helped show the *general direction* in which we were to walk; the fixed object gave us a *focus* that helped us not to drift off course.

Job had his internal compass set. When trouble came, he could endure because he looked inward at that compass of integrity. But Job also needed a fixed point of reference to help him stay on course. Job's fixed point of reference was the character and nature of God. Job could endure because he looked to God, even when it appeared that God had abandoned him.

When Job spoke with his three friends, their "comfort" provided no help at all. Job needed to speak to God. As the incessant speeches of the three friends wore on, Job turned from them to seek out God. In frustration he cried out, "I know as much as you [three friends] do. You are no better than I am. Oh, how I long to speak directly to the Almighty. I want to argue my case with God himself. For you are smearing me with lies. As doctors, you are worthless quacks. Please be quiet! That's the smartest thing you could do" (Job 13:2-5).

Job wanted—needed—to speak with God. But from Job's perspective, God was the Author of his misfortunes. Why, then, seek out God? Ultimately it was a matter of trust. Job didn't understand why God permitted him to suffer, but Job still trusted in God. "God might kill me, but I cannot wait. I am going to argue my case with him. But this is what will save me: that I am not godless. If I were, I would be thrown from his presence" (13:15-16).

I find Job's faith in God remarkable. He did not know of the cosmic struggle causing his pain. (We do!) He did not possess any of God's Word to give him comfort, perspective, or hope. (We do!) He did not know that God had already decreed he would not die. (We do!) He did not know that God would reward his faithfulness and restore his life. (We do!) Job knew far less about God than we do, but he trusted God completely.

At one point Job cried out, "Even now my witness is in heaven. My advocate is there on high. My friends scorn me, but I pour out my tears to God. Oh, that someone would mediate between God and me, as a person mediates between friends" (16:19-21). Job longed for someone in heaven to hear his words and present his case to God.

What Job longed for, we know we have. We have *two* advocates in heaven pleading for us: God the Holy Spirit and God the Son. In Romans 8 the apostle Paul reminded his readers that "the Spirit pleads for us believers in harmony with God's own will" (8:27). The writer of Hebrews described Jesus as the "great High Priest who has gone to heaven" and who "understands our weaknesses" (4:14-15). Because of Jesus' ministry for us, the writer urged his readers to go confidently before God in prayer. "Let us come boldly to the throne of our gracious God. There we will receive his mercy, and we will find grace to help us when we need it" (4:16).

Job endured because he knew God was still seated on his throne, in control of all people, events, and circumstances. Job knew he could continue to trust God, and he knew that God would hear, and eventually act, on his heartfelt cries. Job had no idea when, or how, God would respond. But he endured because he knew God *would* respond, sometime. He just had to hang on till then.

Endurance Comes from Looking Outward

Reading through the book of Job reminds me of the one and only time I drove a car in England. I vividly remember my first *roundabout,* a circular intersection where roads and highways merge. I was seated on the "wrong" side of the car, driving on the "wrong" side of the highway, merging the "wrong" way on this circular roundabout, all the while watching for other cars and the proper exit! I concentrated so much on not hitting other drivers and on staying in the proper lane that I missed the turnoff twice!

Job's three friends drove their dilapidated theological truck onto Job's roundabout and kept going round and round. Same flawed arguments. Same incorrect conclusions. Same self-righteous sense of superiority. These guys were a bunch of jerks! Job finally blurted out, "I have heard all this before. What miserable comforters you are! Won't you ever stop your flow of foolish words? What have I said that makes you speak so endlessly?" (Job 16:2-3).

All right! Give it to them, Job! They deserve it! The last thing we need in our time of struggle is self-appointed sages with simplistic solutions to our difficult problems. In our time of pain and hurt we are tempted to lash out at those around us, and these three buffoons made tempting targets.

In the end God justified Job and condemned the three friends. "I am angry with you [Eliphaz, the "senior partner" of these three stooges] and with your two friends, for you have not been right in what you said about me, as my servant Job was" (42:7). I can almost hear Job saying under his breath, *Way to go, God! Show these morons how wrong they were!*

God ordered the three friends to "take seven young bulls and seven rams and . . . offer a burnt offering for yourselves" (42:8). Then God asked Job to *pray* for his friends. "My servant Job will pray for you, and I will accept his prayer on your behalf" (42:8). I suspect Job's head shot up and furrows lined his brow as he replayed in his mind what God had just said. *What!* You want *me* to serve as the intercessor for my "friends"? These are the ones who have been harassing me!

Christ's disciples must have been as surprised as Job when they heard Jesus tell them, "You have heard that the law of Moses says, 'Love your neighbor' and hate your enemy. But I say, love your enemies! Pray for those who persecute you!" (Matthew 5:43-44). Harboring grudges, nursing bitterness, and holding on to hatred will imprison an individual. Locked in a cell of anger, that person will allow the past to control the future. God commands us to endure the problems and pains of this life, but he does not want our reaction to those problems and pains to hold us hostage.

Sometimes when reading the Bible, we suddenly gain new insight into a passage we have read countless times before. The truth was always there; we just didn't notice it before. I made one such discovery recently in the last chapter of Job. God asked Job to pray for his "friends," and Job did. "When Job prayed for his friends, the Lord restored his fortunes. In fact, the Lord gave him twice as much as before!" (Job 42:10). The King James Version of the Bible, though slightly more poetic, says the same thing. "And the Lord turned the captivity of Job, when he prayed for his friends."

The key to the passage is the timing of God's restoration of Job. I had always assumed God restored Job's health and wealth as soon as Job's encounter with God ended. But Job 42:10 clearly says that God restored Job *when he prayed for his friends.* In looking outward to minister to others, Job experienced God's blessing.

It's all too easy to become self-absorbed when facing problems and troubles. God taught Job (and us) a valuable lesson. One way to endure problems is to look beyond ourselves to others. In ministering to others we will find the strength and endurance to handle our own struggles.

Endurance Comes from Looking Forward

Job looked *inward* for integrity, he looked *upward* for stability, and he looked *outward* for service. All three helped Job endure. But Job looked in one additional direction, and it provided hope. He looked *forward* to the time when God would make all things right!

Job expected to die from the disease devastating his body. But Job could endure because he looked beyond this life to a life that existed beyond the grave. "I know that my Redeemer lives, and that he will stand upon the earth at last. And after my body has decayed, yet in my body I will see God! I will see him for myself. Yes, I will see him with my own eyes. I am overwhelmed at the thought!" (Job 19:25-27).

Job could endure because he somehow sensed life didn't end at death. Remember, Job had none of the Bible! He did not know God's plan for the ages. He didn't comprehend the death and resurrection of God's Son. And he had no detailed knowledge of God's future resurrection or of the new heaven and new earth where all God's people will spend eternity.

Yet, Job instinctively knew there was more to life than just physical existence on this earth. And he knew God would one day make everything right. He could confidently state, "But he knows where I am going. And when he has tested me like gold in a fire, he will pronounce me innocent" (23:10). He could endure because he looked beyond his circumstances to the future.

Run the Race

When I think of endurance, I think of marathon runners. Their grit, determination, and drive are worthy examples of the endurance we ought to display in our lives. The writer of Hebrews compared our spiritual life to a "race that God has set before us" (Hebrews 12:1). He urged us to "run with endurance" (12:1). We need to stay the course. But what are the items on our mental checklist that we must remember in order to run with endurance? The writer focused on the same four items that helped Job endure:

- *Look inward.* "Strip off every weight that slows us down, especially the sin that so easily hinders our progress." (12:1)
- *Look upward.* "We do this by keeping our eyes on Jesus, on whom our faith depends from start to finish." (12:2)
- *Look outward.* "Try to live in peace with everyone, and seek to live a clean and holy life . . . Look after each other so that none of you will miss out on the special favor of God." (12:14-15)
- *Look forward.* "Since we are receiving a kingdom that cannot be destroyed, let us be thankful and

please God by worshiping him with holy fear and awe." (12:28)

Questions to Ponder

We must view the Christian life as a marathon, not a hundred-yard dash. Endurance is essential for surviving the highs and lows of "the race that God has set before us."

1. As you read through this book, did you make any specific commitments to being a man or woman of integrity? Now is the time to look inward and reaffirm your commitment to personal integrity, whatever life brings your way.

2. What are the fixed points you are using to establish your spiritual bearings? Are your eyes fixed on Jesus? on studying his Word? on spending time with him in prayer? Looking beyond your problems to the God who can solve them will help you endure.

3. Who are the people in your life now causing you the most grief? Choose one and pray for him or her this week. Ask God to provide one specific way for you to show kindness to that person. Don't become a prisoner to your anger.

4. Memorize John 14:1-4, and view your problems from an eternal perspective. The problems you face today are only temporary. Heaven is eternal.

We also pray that you will be strengthened with his glorious power so that you will have all the patience and endurance you need. May you be filled with joy, always thanking the Father, who has enabled you to share the inheritance that belongs to God's holy people, who live in the light. (Colossians 1:11-12)

EPILOGUE

Mary Dyer

My family traces its roots back to Colonial New England. Decades ago an aging member of the Dyer family, Jinks Dyer (his real name!), sat down and wrote out all the traditions and history that had been passed down to him by parents, grandparents, aunts, and uncles. I received a copy of this handwritten history, and I found it to be fascinating—skeletons and all!

The first Dyers to come to America, William and Mary Dyer, landed at Boston in 1635. The family background of William and Mary remains shrouded in mystery. Tradition says that Mary Dyer was the only daughter of Sir William Seymour and Arabella Stuart, cousin of King James I of England. The king felt threatened by this marriage and had William Seymour and Arabella imprisoned in the Tower of London. Mary was secretly raised by Arabella's lady-in-waiting. At the age of twenty-two, Mary married William Dyer, a cousin of the woman who raised her. Quite a story! But it gets even better!

Boston in 1635 was a bastion of Puritan worship and law. The Puritans fled to America to seek religious freedom, but they refused to extend that freedom to other religious groups. William and Mary Dyer ran afoul of the authorities when they sided with those who took a less legalistic approach to their faith. Forced to leave Boston, they traveled southwest to a settlement started two years earlier by Roger Williams. That settlement, in what is today Rhode Island, offered William and Mary the opportunity for religious freedom.

Mary Dyer's spiritual pilgrimage continued until she met George Fox, who persuaded her to become a Quaker. From that time on, Mary felt compelled to return to Boston to be a witness to that closed community. Twice she returned to Boston. Both times she was arrested. Her life reads like a tragic novel. Imprisoned, banished, imprisoned again, and finally tried and sentenced to death by hanging.

From the jail where she would one day be led out to be hanged, Mary wrote to the Boston magistrates, "My life not availeth me in comparison to the liberty of the truth." Those words are now inscribed on a bronze statue of Mary Dyer that stands in front of the Boston State House. Mary Dyer passionately believed in the truth of God's Word, and she willingly gave her life for that truth. Was her life in vain?

Ruth Plimpton records the aftermath of Mary Dyer's death—and the effect it had on Edward Wanton, one of the spectators who witnessed her execution.

Edward Wanton vomited in Frog Pond three times before he could mount his steed. As he trotted past the great elm tree, his horse whinnied, reared, and almost threw him to the ground. He pressed his heels and hurried home. Once inside his mother's house, he threw down his musket and halberd. Sinking his head in his arms he sobbed, "Alas Mother! We have been murdering the Lord's people," and taking off his sword, he made a vow never to wear it again. Not long after, he became a member of the Society of Friends and two years later he was arrested for holding Quaker meetings in his house.[1]

What Difference Does One Life Make?

Can one person make a difference? Yes, if that individual is a man or woman of integrity. If that individual shines as a light in a dark world. If that individual displays the character of Jesus Christ in word and deed. God specializes in changing the world one person at a time.

The prophet Micah lived in dark days. Corruption and compromise marked the nation of Judah. "You rulers govern for the bribes you can get; you priests teach God's laws only for a price; you prophets won't prophesy unless you are paid" (Micah 3:11). The nation careened out of control, plunging down a treacherous path that could end only in catastrophe. "So because of you, Mount Zion will be plowed like an open field; Jerusalem will be reduced to rubble! A great forest will grow on the hilltop, where the Temple now stands" (3:12).

Yet God called Micah to be different—to stand as a model of integrity and righteousness. After describing society's moral cesspool, Micah announced his willingness to stand alone for the truth. "But as for me, I am filled with power and the Spirit of the Lord. I am filled with justice and might, fearlessly pointing out Israel's sin and rebellion" (3:8).

But what can one person do alone? How can one individual make a difference? Micah doesn't provide the answer, but another prophet does. A century after Micah, Jeremiah the prophet also stood alone to face a nation collectively spitting in the face of God. On one particular occasion Jeremiah delivered an impassioned message to those gathered in the temple in Jerusalem. When he finished, a crowd seized him. "'Kill him!' they shouted" (Jeremiah 26:8). Many expected a swift trial—and certain death. But some of the older (and wiser!) leaders stepped forward to defend Jeremiah. They compared Jeremiah's words to those spoken a century earlier by Micah.

> Then some of the wise old men stood and spoke to the people there. They said, "Think back to the days when Micah of Moresheth prophesied during the reign of King Hezekiah of Judah. He told the people of Judah, 'This is what the Lord Almighty says: Mount Zion will be plowed like an open field; Jerusalem will be reduced to rubble! A great forest will grow on the hilltop, where the Temple now stands.'" (26:17-18)

Micah's words stood the test of time. People remembered the message long after Micah was gone. But Micah's prophecies had done more than merely fill heads with knowledge. Micah single-handedly changed an entire generation!

After quoting Micah's prophecy of judgment, the elders reminded the mob of the impact Micah's message had made on the people to whom he spoke. "But did King Hezekiah and the people kill him for saying this? No, they turned from their sins and worshiped the Lord. They begged him to have mercy on them. Then the Lord held back the terrible disaster he had pronounced against them. If we kill Jeremiah, who knows what will happen to us?" (26:19).

Micah may have stood alone, but his message had an impact on his nation! Micah's willingness to stand for what was right—to swim against the current—changed an entire generation. God held back his judgment because a nation repented in response to Micah's words and deeds. One man made a difference!

Where Do I Go from Here?

Life brings change. Where you live. Where you work. How you dress. All these can, and often do, change over time. Flexibility and adaptability are two traits that can help us respond to the accelerating rate of change taking place all around us.

But some things must never change. Integrity never goes out of style. Christlike character remains God's standard for those who claim his Son as their Savior. Your commitment to a lifestyle patterned after Jesus Christ must never waver.

The world offers "the good life"; God gives eternal life. The world emphasizes "doing"; God emphasizes "being." The world stresses achievement; God stresses integrity. The world pressures to conform; God works to transform. The world focuses on the outward signs of "success"; God focuses on the inner qualities of the heart.

Like a skilled physician, Chuck Swindoll looks past the symptoms to diagnose the true problem.

> As I wade through the success propaganda written today, again and again the focus of attention is on one's outer self—how smart I can appear, what a good impression I can make, how much I can own or how totally I can control or how fast I can be promoted or . . . or . . . or. Nothing I read—and I mean *nothing*—places emphasis on the heart, the inner being, the seed plot of our thoughts, motives, decisions. Nothing, that is, except Scripture.
>
> Interestingly, the Bible says little about success, but a lot about the heart, the place where true success originates.[2]

Think of this book as a spiritual "stress test." Throughout the book you have been experiencing God's treadmill of integrity. God has been monitoring all your spiritual vital signs, checking for any irregularities. Back in the Great Physician's office, you hear the diagnosis—and prognosis.

The Great Physician notes areas of strength and weakness. Some lifestyle changes are necessary for complete spiritual health. But now the book is finished—the examination is over. As you walk from the office, you know that the decision to change, or not to change, is one that only you can make.

William Longstaff, an English businessman, made a

decision to live a life of integrity and holiness. He wrote a simple poem explaining what living such a life meant to him—and years later his poem, "Take Time to Be Holy," was set to music. This simple poem "may have been the only poem he ever wrote. . . . A businessman at heart, Longstaff wrote no flowery or pious-sounding verses, but these down-to-earth thoughts."[3]

Read Longstaff's words carefully—and make them your own as you decide *now* to live a life of integrity.

Take time to be holy, speak oft with thy Lord;
Abide in Him always, and feed on His Word:
Make friends of God's children; help those who are weak;
Forgetting in nothing His blessing to seek.

Take time to be holy, the world rushes on;
Much time spend in secret with Jesus alone;
By looking to Jesus, like Him thou shalt be;
Thy friends in thy conduct his likeness shall see.

Take time to be holy, let Him be thy guide,
And run not before Him whatever betide;
In joy or in sorrow still follow the Lord,
And, looking to Jesus, still trust in His Word.

Take time to be holy, be calm in thy soul;
Each thought and each motive beneath His control;
Thus led by His Spirit to fountains of love,
Thou soon shalt be fitted for service above.

NOTES

CHAPTER 1

1. Michael Kelly, "Why the President Is in Trouble," *New York Times Magazine,* 31 July 1994.
2. Barbara De Witt, "The Plain Truth about Lying," *Dallas Morning News,* 29 December 1994, C13.
3. Ibid.

CHAPTER 2

1. Bob St. John, "Slip of the Ears Can Leave You Embarrassed," *Dallas Morning News,* 5 March 1989, A37.
2. Jerry Adler et al., "Innocents Lost," *Newsweek,* 14 November 1994, 27.

CHAPTER 4

1. Bob St. John, *The Landry Legend: Grace under Pressure* (Dallas: Word Publishing, 1989), 290–291.
2. Stephen R. Covey, *The 7 Habits of Highly Effective People* (New York: Simon & Schuster, 1989), 92.
3. Kenneth L. Woodward with Susan Miller, "What Is Virtue?" *Newsweek,* 13 June 1994, 39.

CHAPTER 5

1. Richard A. Swenson, *Margin* (Colorado Springs: NavPress, 1992), 115.

CHAPTER 10

1. Bertha Spafford Vester, *Our Jerusalem,* (1950; reprint, Jerusalem: Ariel Publishing House, 1988), 47.
2. These are the handwritten words of the first draft of Spafford's poem as they appear on the stationery of the Brevoort House hotel. Spafford modified the words slightly when the poem was set to music. The most significant change was the final line, which was changed to "'Even so'—it is well with my soul" to continue the theme of Christ's second coming.

EPILOGUE

1. Ruth Plimpton, *Mary Dyer: Biography of a Rebel Quaker* (Boston: Branden Publishing Co., 1994), 188–189.
2. Charles R. Swindoll, *The Quest for Character* (Grand Rapids: Zondervan Publishing House, 1982), 27.
3. William J. Petersen and Randy Petersen provide the background for this hymn in their devotional for May 31 in *The One Year Book of Hymns,* edited by Robert K. Brown and Mark R. Norton (Wheaton, Ill.: Tyndale House Publishers, 1995).